HOUSES OF THE WEST

Architectural Record Series

Apartments, Townhouses, and Condominiums, 2/e
The Architectural Record Book of Vacation Houses, 2/e
Buildings for the Arts
Campus Planning and Design
Great Houses for View Sites, Beach Sites, Sites in the Woods,
   Meadow Sites, Small Sites, Sloping Sites, Steep Sites,
   and Flat Sites
Hospitals and Health Care Facilities, 2/e
Houses Architects Design for Themselves
Houses of the West
Interior Spaces Designed by Architects
Office Building Design, 2/e
Places for People: Hotels, Motels, Restaurants, Bars, Clubs,
   Community Recreation Facilities, Camps, Parks, Plazas, Playgrounds
Recycling Buildings: Renovations, Remodelings, Restorations,
   and Reuses
Techniques of Successful Practice, 2/e

Architectural Record Series Books

Ayers: Specifications for Architecture, Engineering, and Construction
Feldman: Building Design for Maintainability
Heery: Time, Cost, and Architecture
Heimsath: Behavioral Architecture
Hopf: Designer's Guide to OSHA
Portman and Barnett: The Architect as Developer
Redstone: The New Downtowns

HOUSES OF THE WEST

BY ELISABETH KENDALL THOMPSON, FAIA

AN ARCHITECTURAL RECORD BOOK

McGraw-Hill Book Company

New York   St. Louis   San Francisco   Auckland   Bogotá   Düsseldorf   Johannesburg   London   Madrid   Mexico
Montreal   New Delhi   Panama   Paris   São Paulo   Singapore   Sydney   Tokyo   Toronto

The editors for this book were Jeremy Robinson
and Sue Cymes. The designer was
Andrew Steigmeier.
The production supervisors were Elizabeth Dineen
and Teresa Leaden
The book was set in Optima and Memphis by
Monotype Composition Company, Inc.
Printed and bound by Halliday Lithograph
Corporation.

**Library of Congress Cataloging in Publication
Data**

Thompson, Elisabeth Kendall.
  Houses of the West.

  "An Architectural record book."
  Includes index.
  1. Architecture, Domestic—The West.
2. Architecture, Anonymous—The West.
I. Title.
NA7223.T48 1978   728'.09182'1   77-15106
ISBN 0-07-002339-5

1234567890 HDHD 78654321098

CONTENTS

in the Suburbs   91

Section III: Houses in Vacation Places for Occasional Use
in the Woods   131

PREFACE: THE WESTERN HOUSE

The Western states, in common with all the other states of this country, contain so many types and styles of houses that no single kind can be said to "typify" the Western house. The West is as filled with meretricious derivatives of historic styles as any other part of the United States, and as guilty of despoiling the landscape with tract development. If at times it has had the best in residential architecture, it also has had the worst.

But there is a particular kind of house, indigenous to the West, whose clear and direct relationship to site and to way of living has made it, from its beginnings over a century ago, a vital and far-reaching influence on residential design. More an approach to design than a set of rules, an individual expression of an individual response to people and place, this kind of Western house is timeless, contemporary in every period of time. It relies on no specific forms and requires no specified details. Its use of locally available materials is commonsense, not stylistic. The individualism of this kind of Western house is the only "ism" of which it partakes.

There have never been many of these houses at any one time, but what they were has made up, to those who sought them out, for the smallness of their number. For a while, from the mid-1870s through the end of the century, such houses were concentrated in the hills around San Francisco Bay, designed for clients of adventurous spirit—writers, artists, professors at the University of California. But good ideas will not be localized, and the idea of a vernacular architecture spread to other areas, took root and developed its own regional expression. In subtle ways, certain similarities and differences were observable—for instance, Bay Area houses were more like northwest houses than like the houses designed for the southerly parts of the West. The vernacular approach allowed for, even encouraged, regional differences in design.

In the hands of sensitive architects, the houses that developed from these beginnings became a major influence in freeing design for two important changes it was to face increasingly: a growing informality in living patterns, and the elimination, from economic pressure, of unnecessary spaces in houses. What this kind of house did was to prove that it was possible to live with elegance and comfort in a greatly simplified house. In the Depression years, this was an important economic consideration, for architects as well as for their newly-poor clients, for it kept alive the practice of architecture when the only other generally active building type was the publicly funded building. The once-wealthy, newly-poor client, no longer able to maintain a large house and a staff of servants, but still able to live comfortably, wanted a house which would make it possible to live, within a drastically reduced income, without sacrificing entirely the niceties to which he and his family were accustomed. The Western houses of the late 1920s and 1930s, designed to meet this new way of living— simple but elegant, informal but sophisticated, servantless but easily cared for— were prophetic: today, the simple, the informal, the servantless way of life is the American norm.

That architects and builders, professionals and amateurs, in other parts of this country (and, indeed, in other parts of the world) have chosen to emulate this kind of house points up how close to the public need its concepts, based in indigenous ways, were—and still are. That so many imitations were done without any understanding of the essential principle that made the vernacular Western house an attractive and livable solution to mid-twentieth-century living is more than unfortunate, for the results rarely, if ever, even approximated the character and quality of the prototype.

Now, the essentials of the house, not its embellishment, are again the focus of attention, with pressure as in that earlier day from the economics of the times. The secret of the West's vernacular house—if so open and natural an approach to design could be a secret —has always been that it dealt with the essentials of what Lewis Mumford, discussing the work of Bay Area architects in 1948, called its "humane way."

The houses selected for this book are of very recent date and yet they, too, in their individual and up-to-date ways, exemplify the same approach to design. Although outwardly these houses resemble their antecedents little if at all, it is easy to recognize in them the same respect for the character of the site and the same advantageous use of it; the same design acknowledgment of climatic and regional differences; the same easy come-and-go from house to out-of-doors; the same sympathetic and sensible use of local materials; and the same satisfaction of client needs without the dogma of style.

Simplicity, harmony with the natural environment, and lack of pretense are the special virtues of these houses, and these are indeed virtues of value. Even the largest and most expensive of these houses is not pretentious; even the most elegant permits informal living. The geometry of their forms is unforced. The affinity of house to site is a joy to behold and even more to experience.

These houses are *of* the West as well as in the West, and, subtle as may be the distinction, they are different from the houses of other sections of the country. It was not for difference, however, that they were selected for this book. Their inclusion is, rather, evidence of the timelessness of undogmatic design, and of the tradition of bold and direct response to the users of the house—its inhabitants, their guests, their helpers—to the way they will use it, to the advantages or disadvantages, of climate, and to the challenge of using the land on which the house stands without destroying it.

Elisabeth Kendall Thompson FAIA

HOUSES OF THE WEST

SECTION I

HOUSES FOR HILL SITES

The house on a hill, in town or suburb, is almost always an interesting house, the more so because of its sloping site, which gives it an outlook over what lies below and makes possible unusual and varying interior spatial relationships. The steeper the slope, however, the more difficult can be the problem of building on it. A safe and secure anchorage is basic. Once, a 30-degree slope would have been rejected as too steep to build on, but because even these lots are becoming scarce, especially in urban areas, they have a new attraction, and their problems have to be dealt with.

The comon factor in hill houses in the West is the slope of the site, not the degree of urbanization of the locality. For without a strong townhouse tradition (found only in San Francisco, which was rebuilt in this manner after the earthquake and fire had destroyed earlier buildings) what is built in cities and what is built in suburbs do not differ greatly. City lots can be wooded as much as suburban lots, and flattening out a lot can be as necessary in the suburbs as in town. In the sections which follow (Houses for Hill Sites in the city, pages xiii–18, and in the suburbs, pages 19–56), a broad range of houses deals with hill sites of many types and degrees of difficulty, and a handsome house in Albuquerque, which is designed to collect the sun's heat for space and water heating, is shown.

IN THE CITY

Anchored on a ridge among stands of tall evergreen trees, the house takes full advantage of some of the most splendid views to be found anywhere in the Northwest. To do so, it makes a virtue of irregularity, ordering it and controlling it by the requirements of the vistas and the functions of the interior spaces.

Starting with a steeply contoured site southwest of Portland—a site that offers arresting views to the north and northwest—architects Martin and Soderstrom planned a complex, three-level house for a couple with two teenage daughters. Dominated by a massive masonry core, the house is organized so that support spaces are located in the core or on the blind side while prime spaces open generously to the view of valley floor and mountains beyond. The necessary degree of intra-family privacy is achieved by sensible vertical and horizontal zoning (see floor plans and transverse section on facing page).

What is perhaps most appealing about the house is the way that consistent detailing and use of materials have united an almost unmanageable assortment of projections, intersections, roof slopes and window openings. Visual rhythms are all but absent. But this complexity of plan and massing is clearly not the result of vagrant afterthought. It is an integral part of the planning and contributes a spirit of relaxed informality. This is a house that depends for much of its success on energetic but unifying detail and really superior craftsmanship. Happily, it got both.

The interiors are designed and executed with the same respect for material and attention to detail. Cedar siding is carried inside for continuity where it contrasts in color and texture with gypsum board and concrete block. Windows are double glazed and trimmed with fir. The over-all result is a series of spaces that are comfortable, view oriented, and—even on a gray, winter day—invested with visual warmth.

PRIVATE RESIDENCE, Portland Oregon. Architects: *Martin & Soderstrom;* structural engineers: *Werner Storch & Associates, Inc.;* general contractor: *Architectural Construction Company;* interiors: *Robert Weller Design in collaboration with Martin & Soderstrom.*

All interior photos: Ron Green

7

2

The plans contain several unexpected or personal elements. Over the entrance stair, a small playroom anticipates the arrival of grandchildren. It is reached only by an accommodation ladder from the stair itself. On the lower level, light is introduced into the back of the family room by an unusual device—an inside window into a daughter's bedroom. A loom room, part of the upstairs master bedroom suite, is used by the owner's wife. Finally, extending out from under the detached garage, the owner has a workshop turned out toward the timbered valley. The use of sapwood in the cedar siding, both inside and out, lends lively visual interest. Further interest is achieved by decks that extend living and dining spaces toward the view.

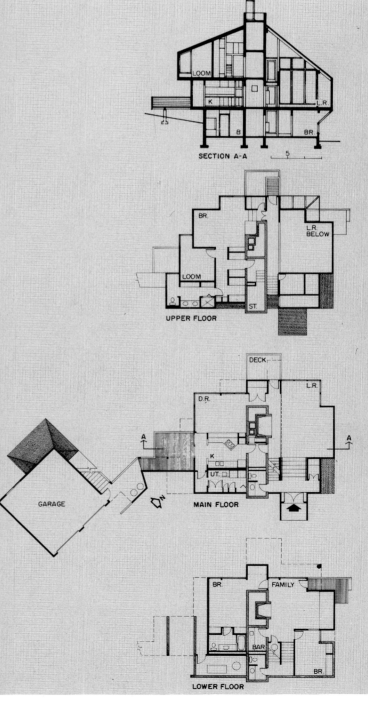

SECTION A-A

UPPER FLOOR

MAIN FLOOR

LOWER FLOOR

Remo Pratini photos except as noted

Edmund Burger

Patricia Coplans' hillside house in San Francisco rises in a conspiracy of angled planes and projections to overlook Golden Gate Park and the Pacific Ocean. The projecting bay windows are part of a local residential tradition but the sloping window walls (photos right) are a direct response to particular site conditions and the architect-owner's desire to capture as much sunlight as possible on this steeply contoured north slope.

The plan is compact and simply ordered in spite of the visual complications created by the pro-jections. The living room occupies the north end of the house over the garage and is overlooked, in turn, by a gallery-level guest bedroom. Master bedroom and bath occupy the second floor over the kitchen. The sloping glass roof of the dining area frames a view up the slope of tall stands of eucalyptus. A central entry hall, also skylighted, is reached from the garage below or by a winding outdoor stair on the west side of the house.

Finish materials are sympa-thetically selected and detailed with skill. Exterior walls are west-ern cedar nailed up in diagonals that echo the slope of the site in two directions. Interior partitions are gypsum board over wood studs; flooring is teak parquet for the living room and clay tile for dining room and kitchen. Rich accents, like the marble fireplace surround, are used sparingly. A dark red baked enamel finish, used on all gutters, down-spouts, window sash corner details and roof, contrasts warmly with the cedar siding, and gives the house a crisp, firm-edged angularity. This linear emphasis is restated inside in the window and door trim as in the unusually crisp and elegant sky-light details.

The Coplans house is invested with a stimulating spatial charac-ter—a character that is personal but not aberrant, a character that does not dissolve with the second or third look.

Architect and *owner:* PATRICIA A. COPLANS of Burger and Coplans. *Location:* San Francisco, Califor-nia. *Engineers:* Geoffrey Barrett (structural); James Peterson (me-chanical). *General contractor:* Pa-tricia Coplans.

The furnishings in the Coplans' house are a mixture of built-ins and modern classics in chrome, cane and leather. The relative formality of many of these pieces is surprising but no problems of compatibility seem to arise.

Large skylights in many spaces flood the house with light but glazing is tinted for protection against the sun's direct rays.

5

Building a new house in an old neighborhood poses special problems of compatibility with nearby existing houses and at the same time, the problems of obtaining the kind of character and amenity that the owners of the new house want for themselves. In this Seattle house, built in an established neighborhood of fairly high density, architect Philip Jacobson has provided for himself and his family a contemporary house suited to their needs and making the most of the site, without doing violence to the form and character of the area. The new house adopts the pitched roof of surrounding houses but uses it in a highly individual way, achieving a sense of simplicity in its long, low uncomplicated line. The palette of materials used on the exterior is small: all-white stucco to give continuity and, again, simplicity to the exterior forms, and asphalt shingles on the roof for the same basic reasons. Inside, the same careful use of a few materials minimizes the visual complexity of the non-rectilinear, varied spaces organized around a central stairway. The off-white walls allow for display of art and for strong color accents in wall hangings, area rugs and furniture. Elegant detailing—in window and door jambs, sills, wall bases, book shelves, fireplace, alcoves for art, and in the sauna and its skylight— are handled with such simplicity that they in no way distract from the basic simplicity of the interior with its variety of spaces—from large, high and open, to small, intimate and enclosed. As much natural light as possible is admitted, both directly and indirectly, to minimize the darkness of winter days. For bright days, wood slat roller blinds on windows and an exterior vinyl roller awning on the skylight protect from solar radiation. All artificial light is indirect.

Since the site has a fine view of Lake Washington, Mount Rainier and the Cascade Mountains, the living room opens toward this view, and its deck, like that of the master bedroom, acts as an extension of the room toward a private landscaped area.

Architect: Philip L. Jacobson
   3935 51st N.E.
   Seattle, Washington
Owners: Mr. and Mrs. Philip L. Jacobson
Location: Seattle, Washington
Contractor: Tom Paulsell Construction Co.
Photographers: Hugh Stratford;
   Philip Jacobson

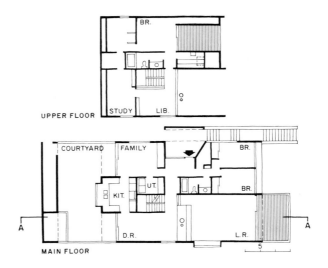

UPPER FLOOR   STUDY   LIB.   BR.

MAIN FLOOR   COURTYARD   FAMILY   BR.   KIT.   U.T.   BR.   D.R.   L.R.   A — A
5

Form, line, color and texture are handled with great simplicity to achieve continuity from exterior to interior, and to allow for a contemporary expression of the owners' wishes and needs.

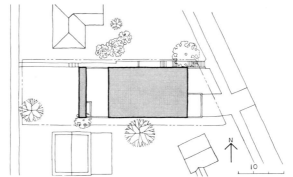
N
10

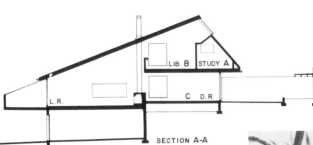

SECTION A-A

The spaces of the house are varied in form as in size, deriving interest from their location under the roof which is expressed on the interior more than usual. The long slope of the cedar plank ceiling and off-white walls of the living room (opposite page) make it the most dramatic interior space, but small enclosed spaces such as those shown above and at right have individuality of a different kind. Brick pavers in the dining room (below) are a visual continuance of the brick paths outside. Natural light fills the balcony which overhangs the living room and, along with the vertical line of the fireplace flues, emphasizes the volume of this room.

A

B

C

Julius Shulman photos

The Heidemann residence outside Los Angeles, by Pulliam Matthews and Associates, is built into the flank of a hill on a three-quarter-acre site that drops nearly 50 feet corner to corner. The slope, and the owner's desire to have both a tennis court and a swimming pool on the property, sharply limited the building area available. A reasonably compact, two-level solution was the result.

An open stairwell (page 13, middle) separates the active and quiet areas of the house. Game room and living room are oriented to the south and overlook both pool and tennis court. Kitchen, library and bedrooms face north. Parking is under the lower living area. Above the concrete podium, which extends in the form of a long retaining wall to embrace the tennis court, the house is framed in wood and finished in heavily-textured stucco. Windows are set back two to six feet from the outside wall to protect against Southern California's intense sunlight.

The interiors, somewhat formal in terms of furnishing and dressy in terms of finish, are executed with consistent skill. A brown, marble facing on the fireplace wall is an elegant accent to the plaster partitioning and oak flooring. Chrome handrails lend sparkle to the skylighted, central stairwell and offer a design theme that is picked up again in the furniture. In the living room, sculpture, planting and high-contrast graphics combine to provide a strong visual impact to a deliberately understated white-on-white scheme.

Careful massing and attention to planning and detail, inside and out, give the Heidemann house an unusual richness, clarity and interest. The Heidemann house has its own distinct character but belongs, at the same time, to a Los Angeles tradition that dates back to Irving Gill and perhaps earlier.

Architects: PULLIAM, MATTHEWS AND ASSOCIATES—Jaswant Bhogal, project architect. *Owner:* Bernard Heidemann. *Location:* Beverly Hills, California. *Structural engineer:* Norman J. Epstein. *Landscape architects:* Robert Joseph Clark Associates. *Interior designer:* Signe Holechek. *General contractor:* R. C. Wheeler

The crisp white planes of the interiors reflect the light beautifully and also serve as excellent neutral backgrounds for graphic and sculptural display. The end wall of the living room (photo opposite page, bottom) is designed to house hi-fi equipment.

A skylighted, central stairwell (photo below) separates the living-dining areas from the rest of the house. Behind this stairwell, a small pantry links kitchen to dining area creating an easy pattern of circulation.

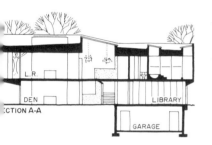

L.R.

DEN | LIBRARY

CTION A-A

GARAGE

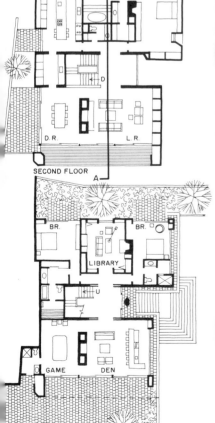

A

KIT. | BR.

D

D.R. | L.R.

SECOND FLOOR

A

BR. | BR.

LIBRARY

GAME | DEN

FIRST FLOOR

5

Eight concrete piers support this house clear of the steep slope of the hill on which it stands, much as *pilotis* support the buildings of the clearly defined International Style. But this house is no more a part of that style than it is of a mythical Bay Area Style. It relates very strongly, nevertheless, to the site, for not only is the hillside very steep, posing special problems for construction, but its two top strata are unstable, making the independent structure an eminently practical solution. (The piers are drilled five feet into bedrock and are connected by concrete grade beams to form a rigid frame for the 48- by 32-foot platform on which the house is built.) This solution also preserves most of the vegetation on the site, and the house seems to grow out of the site. The exterior is of redwood board, applied vertically and shiplapped, and redwood is also used as panelling in the library at one end of the living room and on the sloping ceilings. A broad bridge, which serves as both entrance walk and driveway, connects the house to the street. Only the master bedroom suite is on the entry level; the main rooms are all on the floor below. From the two-story living room and the decks at each end are splendid Bay views.

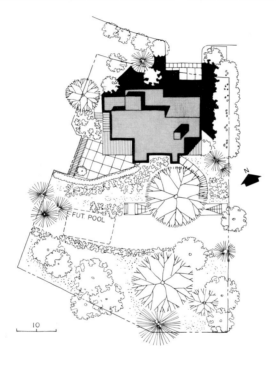

UPPER FLOOR

LOWER FLOOR

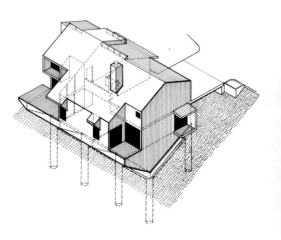

RESIDENCE FOR MR. & MRS. DONALD C. GEDDES, Oakland, California. Architect: *Donald C. Geddes.* Structural engineer: *Peter C. Tardos.* Contractor: *Ronson Construction Co.*

Merg Ross photos

SIXTH LEVEL

FIFTH LEVEL

STUDIO

FAMILY

DECK UPPER D.R.

FOURTH LEVEL
(ENTRY LEVEL)

L.R.

DECK

KIT.

D.R.

DECK

THIRD LEVEL

BR.

BR.

LAUN. ELEV.

BR.

SECOND LEVEL

SHOP

DECK

BR.

FIRST LEVEL

RECREATION

Allan McCoy photos

The genesis of this design was a wedge-shaped lot with a spectacular view, but sloping to a degree which almost signalled unbuildability. The solution was a structure built in parts elsewhere and trucked to the site. There a trestle was built at street level at the top, and this became a platform for the crane which lowered the pieces one by one into their proper positions. Later, the trestle became a car park for the finished house.

The house is made of three tall towers, connected at some levels and separate at others. The smallest of these towers twines around an elevator shaft. The other towers hold at various levels the living room, children's bedroom and bath, and a workshop in the one, and a studio, family room, kitchen-dining room, the master bedroom, the guest room, and a game room

in the other. The frame of the house is a freestanding skeleton which receives no structural help from the wall panels; its members are glue-laminated wood and were pre-cut, pre-drilled, pre-stained and numbered for position. When the skeleton had been erected on concrete footing pads (in five-days' time) diagonal tie rods were added and adjusted to align the structure to receive the wall panels.

These were shop-built of 2 by 4 framing and pre-stained cedar siding, then dropped into place by the crane and bolted onto the frame from inside (in barely four more working days). All the installation was done from the inside.

The completed house is a straightforward, ingenious solution to a taxing site problem.

The obvious disadvantage of a house which is organized vertically

is that the rooms on any one floor are isolated from all the others. Here the architect has countered the practical disadvantages by providing space for an elevator, and lessened the psychological ones, for example, by piercing an open shaft from the kitchen-dining room on the main level all the way up past the family room to the studio at the very top of one of the towers. On the other hand he has also turned disadvantage to advantage, by carefully arranging rooms where isolation is desirable on different levels or in different towers from each other, and from the more public spaces.

Architect: JAMES OLIVER of James Oliver Architects & Associates. *Location:* Portland, Oregon. *Engineers:* Frank Honey & Associates. *Contractor:* Malcolm Merino.

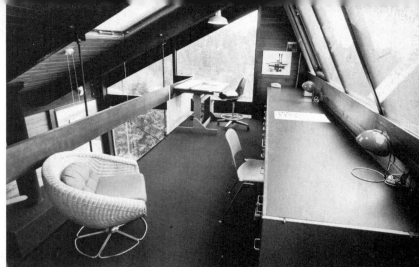

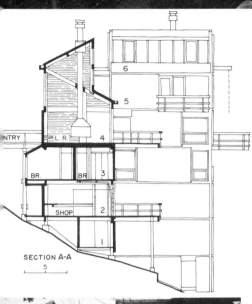

SECTION A-A

5

The entrance to the house (above) is across a bridge which leads to the main public rooms inside. The kitchen-dining room (above left) is open to the studio tucked under the roof (above right). The living room (right) is lit from above by a large light scoop and opens onto a deck and a splendid view.

6 STUDIO

5 FAMILY

4 KITCHEN-DINING

3 BR.

2 BR.

ELEV.

RECREATION 1

SECTION B-B

STOR.

SECTION I
HOUSES
FOR HILL
SITES

IN THE
SUBURBS

In this house, basically simple, are qualities far from simple to attain which give it a distinction beyond the aspiration of most small houses. It has a plainness like that of Shaker houses, and a clarity, timeless but characteristic of the work of its architect, Joseph Esherick. Set on a steep hillside which had been badly graded by a previous owner, the house is T-shaped, with the cross bar containing all the rooms but the studio (which also acts as a third bedroom). The quality of light in the houses he designs is important to Joe Esherick: he speaks of designing light, not windows, and here he has provided the principal spaces with unusual and beautiful light, changing through the day and through the seasons, since light is reflected from the hill behind the house, its color influenced by the color of the grass, green in spring, later buckskin.

Architects: Esherick Homsey Dodge and Davis. *Owners:* Mr. and Mrs. Daniel Romano. *Location:* Kentfield, California. *Contractor:* Skaggs Construction Company.

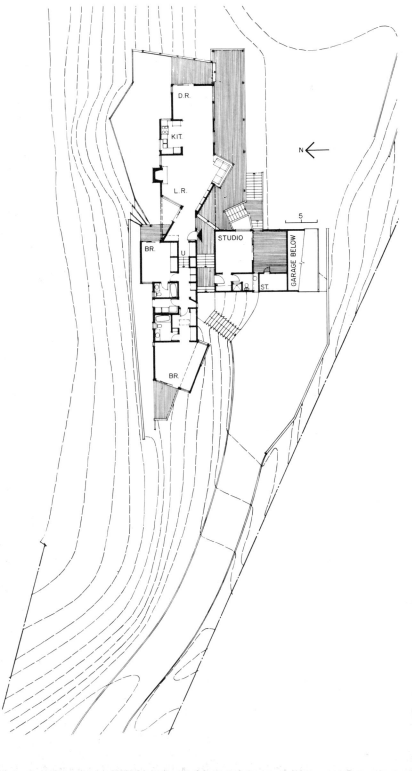

Robert Brandeis photos

This very special and especially dramatic house sits at the edge of a rocky ridge in Palm Springs, California. In some ways, it looks as if it grew there; in other ways it has all the man-made strength of a hill-top fortress.

Designed by architect John Lautner for interior designer Arthur Elrod, the house has almost 6,000 square feet of living space in five rooms all on one level. Most spectacular of the spectaculars is the 60-foot-diameter living room—partially indoors, partially outdoors, and all covered by a

glass and concrete dome. The photos directly above best show the dome inside and out. The poured-in-place, post-tensioned compression ring is supported by the fireplace, the pylon near the pool (photo top left) and the slenderest of columns—which all around the house seem to float the massive concrete roof as if it were polystyrene. Radiating inward from the ring are nine concrete sections with triangular spaces between. Two of these spaces are infilled with clear glass creating sky-windows, the others have triangular copper

wedges with glass clerestories that let light into every section of the big room. The glass in the big view window is mitred and epoxy-glued so that there are no interruptions in the 160-degree view to the valley floor.

As the plan left shows, the kitchen is partitioned off under the big roof. Entered off the living room on the view side is the enormous master bedroom-study-office suite, with dressing room beyond. Along the view wall in this area, some of the great rocks of the site come through the glass

Spectacular views open off all the flowing spaces of the house. Far left, the pool terrace off the living room; this page, left, the dining area near the big fireplace, the stairs—leading through natural site rock—to the sculpture garden, the master bath. Below, left to right: the entryway, a view from the drive, and a broad view of the living room.

wall, which is carefully fitted over them. Across the entryway is a small suite for guests, overlooking a sculpture garden, which in turn opens to the garage.

Throughout, the concrete surfaces are textured by the form boards. The other materials used extensively—copper, rich woods and fabrics, textured rugs, and slate —create a contrasting warmth.

Residence for Arthur Elrod, Palm Springs, California. Architect: *John Lautner;* interior designer: *Arthur Elrod Associates, Inc.;* engineer: *Richard R. Bradshaw, Inc.;* contractor: *Wally Niewiadomski*

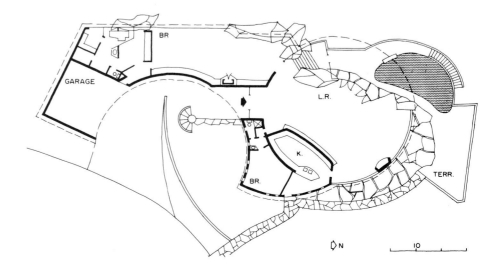

A dramatic entrance stairwell—where fast growing trees and plants create an interior garden effect—is an ingenious solution to the problem of a steeply sloping site. At the same time, the stairwell provides an interesting focus for the main living areas. The device of a raised roof with a band of clerestory glass over the stairwell and dining area is skillfully employed to bring extra light and space into the center of a relatively small house. A handsome stand of eucalyptus trees flanks one side of the site which can be glimpsed through these clerestory windows.

Of simple wood frame construction, this house—designed by the architect for himself and his family—makes substantial use of redwood for exterior and some interior walls and for the trellis which effectively screens exposed glass areas from the sun and also gives shade to an outdoor deck.

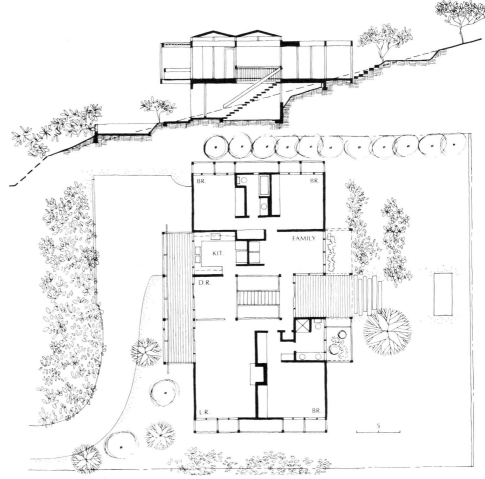

Some well-grown groups of trees on the southern and western sides of the lot protect the house from the heat of the late afternoon sun. An expansive view of the Los Angeles skyline is fully exploited by glass walls in the living room, dining room and kitchen. A patio and terraced slopes at the rear of the lot make a pleasant playground for the two children, who can be easily supervised from the family room which overlooks this area.

Careful zoning allows plenty of living and entertaining space for the adults without conflicting with the children's activities. The children's bedrooms at one end of the house are separated by the kitchen and family room from the main living areas.

A carport and turning area have been cut into the hillside below the house and a steeply sloping driveway leads down to the street.

Architect and *owner:* Young Woo.
Location: Los Angeles, California.
Structural engineer: Tom Woodward.
Contractors: Colletta & Edgley.

Philip Molten photos

Within the simplest imaginable structural framework of this small (under 1,000 square feet) house, architect J. Alexander Riley has created an extraordinary variety of indoor and outdoor spaces. Essentially, as is best seen in the plan and photo at right, the house is made of two flatroofed units set seven feet apart and bridged by a handsomely framed pitched roof set above twin clerestories that pour light into the center of the house, even though it is on a northeastern slope.

That roof is one of four elements that give distinction and interest to what—in less sensitive hands—could have been quite ordinary. The second design device was staggering the ends of the elements—on both the entry and view ends of the plan—to eliminate any sense of boxiness. Third: dropping the living room floor three steps, and leaving it open to the dining room and kitchen to add a sense of spaciousness. Finally, while the house is of the simplest construction, with posts, single-thickness walls of 2¼- by 6-inch cedar and a single-thickness 2 by 6 cedar roof—great attention was paid to the detailing. Note for example the mitered corners of the clerestory structure (photo right) and the simple-to-fabricate but effective detailing of the interior (photos next page).

Architect and *owner:* J. Alexander Riley. *Location:* Inverness, California. *Contractor:* Jean Madill Burroughs.

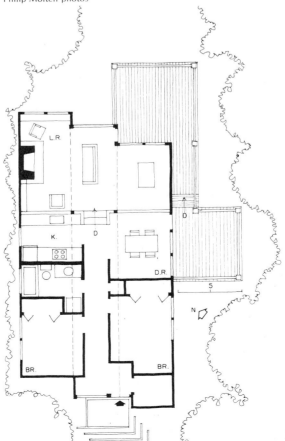

On the interiors, the simple wood framing is clearly expressed, with a small but effective amount of trim and special detailing. The photo (far right) shows the main view wall, with the deck beyond. At right, a view from the living room to the dining room and kitchen three steps above. The kitchen-living room, photo below, emphasizes the changes in scale and room shape worked out within, again, an essentially simple framework.

This warm, comfortable three-level house, with a structure formed by a series of tall Y-shaped "trees," was designed on a moderate budget for a young Colorado family. The owners wanted a house that would affirm its natural mountain setting. Aside from their obvious connotation, the architect felt that the "trees" relate to the forms of many mining structures still seen in the mountains west of Denver.

Made by sandwiching 2 x 6s, 2 x 10s, and 2 x 12s, the "trees" were fabricated on the ground, then hoisted into position. Because the house is anchored to the ground only by the trees, site grading and foundation work were kept to a minimum. The exterior balconies, which are suspended from the structure by cables, seem to float over the site.

The living, dining and library areas are continuous on the entrance level to provide an open space for the full 42-foot width of the house. The balcony-bridge connects the stair with the parents' bedroom and dressing area, bath, utility, and guest rooms. On the below-grade level, open on one side because of the ground slope, are two children's bedrooms closed off by folding doors. Opened, the doors provide another 42-foot area to be used for play on stormy days.

Windows, placed high on the facade, let light into the house while keeping the interior private from the street (see photo below).

The exterior materials are rough-sawn cedar siding, with fir posts and beams. Cedar is used again in the interior along with white plaster board for the walls, and quarry tile for the floors.

Architects: Ream, Quinn & Associates— project design: James T. Ream, 1761 Green Street, San Francisco. Owners: Mr. and Mrs. Peter Lipman; associate architects: David L. Van Wormer and Childress; structural engineers: Ketchum, Konkel, Ryan & Hastings; contractor: Burton A. Payne.

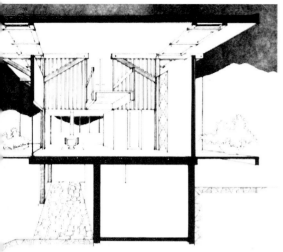

Set on a steep hillside facing the Rocky Mountains, this house achieves the sense of sheltered warmth desired by its young owners without sacrificing any of the view. Standing outside on the balcony (see photo left), which is hung from a system of structural "trees" by steel cables, would be an invigorating experience at any time. On the inside, two large open areas give a feeling of spaciousness.

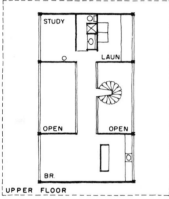

UPPER FLOOR

STUDY

LAUN

OPEN   OPEN

BR.

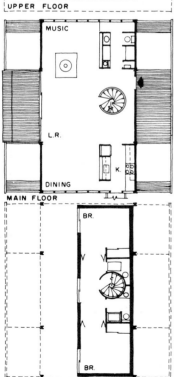

MAIN FLOOR

MUSIC

L.R.

DINING   K.

LOWER FLOOR   5

BR.

BR.

Roger Ewy photos

It is a rare site—the tip of Belvedere Island—with unrivaled views across the Bay to Sausalito and San Francisco. The building area is a narrow strip at the edge of cliffs that tumble down to the water's edge. Specimen pines, their brooding profiles shaped by the prevailing wind, were carefully preserved. The rock itself is deteriorating so caissons were sunk 12 feet to provide a stable foundation. Over these caissons, the architects built a really remarkable house: generously proportioned in its spaces, rambling in its organization, romantic in its images, luxuriant in its details. Living room, dining room, kitchen, master bedroom and rathskeller are all pivoted around a central courtyard on the main level and all of these spaces are linked by a long, skylighted gallery. The level below contains a library, guest quarters and a garage, which is covered with a foot of topsoil to form an exterior yard and garden above. The uppermost level is given over to children's rooms with provisions to accommodate a governess.

The house is designed in what the architects called "the Carmel/Big Sur/Monterey mood," with pitched roofs, wide overhangs, indigenous materials and details that show a great respect for these materials as well as pride in the work of the hands that fashioned them. The collection of furnishings, many pieces inherited from the owner's grandmother, show much the same spirit.

Most remarkable of all, perhaps, is the subtlety with which this 6000-square-foot house is sculpted into the hill.

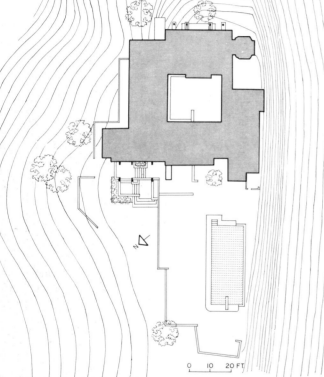

0 10 20 FT

Architects: Callister, Payne & Bischoff
  project architects:
  Alfred Morrissette and John Pryor
  1865 Mar West
  Tiburon, California
Private residence
Location: Belvedere, California
Engineers:
  Shapiro, Okino, Hom
  & Associates (structural)
  Harding, Miller, Lawson
  & Associates (site)
Interior design consultant:
  Anthony Hail Studio
Contractor: Olin Construction
Photographer: Philip Molten

LOWER FLOOR

GARAGE

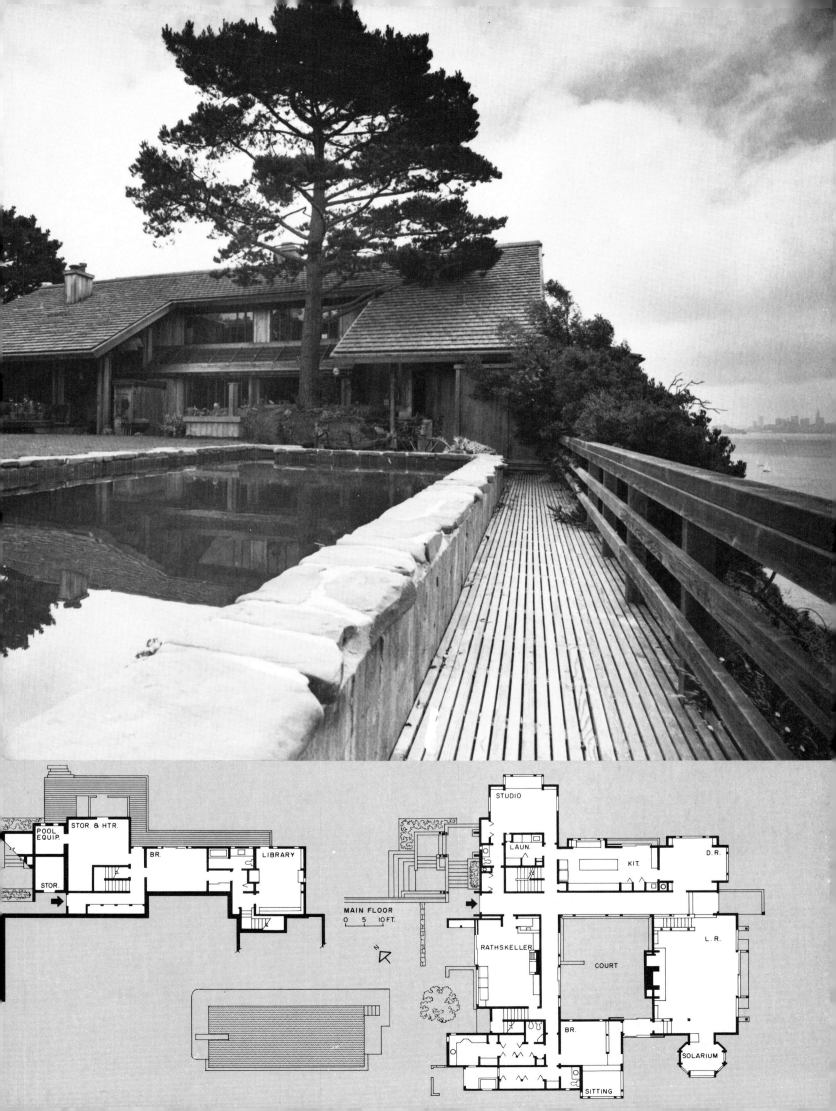

POOL EQUIP.

STOR & HTR.

STOR.

BR.

LIBRARY

MAIN FLOOR
0 5 10 FT.

N

STUDIO

LAUN.

KIT.

D. R.

RATHSKELLER

COURT

L. R.

BR.

SOLARIUM

SITTING

The range of primary finish materials inside is controlled: cedar siding for paneling, waxed slate for some floors, pine boards for others, plastic for skylights. Outside, the house is clad in random width cedar boards laid up vertically and the roof is covered in concrete shingle.

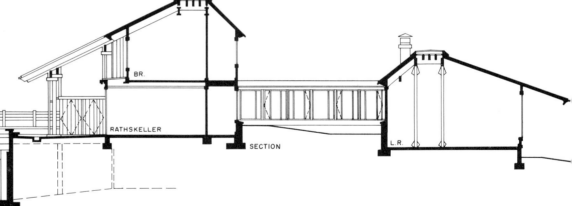

GARAGE

BR.

RATHSKELLER

SECTION

L.R.

At an elevation of over 6,400 feet, this eight-acre site in the Sandia Mountains overlooks in a broad sweep the Rio Grande Valley and distant Mount Taylor to the west. For people who love the outdoors, it is a superb site, and Predock strove to maximize this potential by providing outdoor spaces in the plan for dining, recreation and watching wildlife on the flank of the adjacent mountain.

The main entry at the east, under the sloping solar roof, falls on a long axis that opens across a covered deck toward Mount Taylor. The main spaces of the house lie just off this axis in a fan arrangement that uses a central circular column as a common radius (see plan, lower level) and produces the circular form seen in the exterior photo at right. The kitchen/family room acts as a transition space, both functionally and geometrically, between the living room and the garage. Upstairs are bedrooms and a study that share a small but colorful roof garden.

On the critical faces of the house, Predock has screened out the bright sun with deep overhangs or narrow slit windows. The 950 square feet of solar collectors, inclined at 45 degrees, are part of a flat plate system that uses ethylene glycol as a medium. The solution is circulated from the collectors to a heat exchanger, then to a 6,000-gallon hot-water storage tank. Water in storage is pumped to fan coil units for space heating. Parallel systems are used to meet domestic hot-water demands—and to heat a swimming pool (not shown in plan).

On a site so free of tree cover, in a region so sunny year round, the solar application seems sensible and efficient. The architect reports that about 80 per cent of the heat demand (both space and water) should be met by the solar system and that the "recapture time" for initial costs should be less than 15 years. Increased fuel costs could shorten this period significantly.

In its massing, the house responds to the traditional architectural forms of the region, and the admittedly difficult geometry of arc segments and triangles is sufficiently resolved to create highly interesting spaces and forms that fit this high desert site.

Architect: Antoine Predock
   300 12th Street, N.W.
   Albuquerque, New Mexico
Engineers:
   Randy Holt Associates (structural)
   Bridgers & Paxton (mechanical)
Contractor: Homes by Marilyn
Photographer: Joshua Freiwald

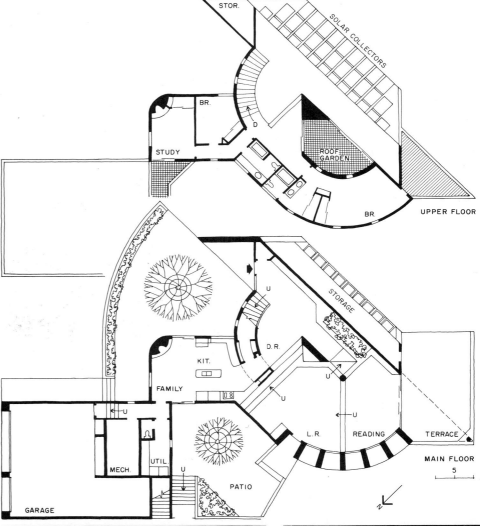

UPPER FLOOR

MAIN FLOOR

36

The principal interior finishes are oak strips for floors and gypsum board for walls and ceilings. Horizontal support members are either concrete or laminated wood beams.

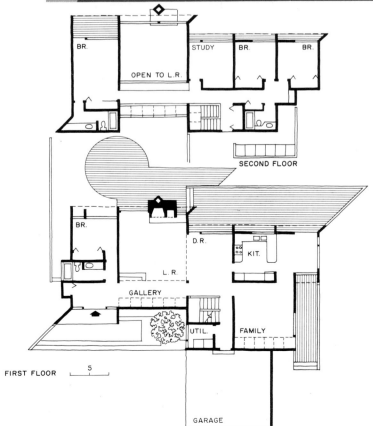

BR.

OPEN TO L.R.

STUDY   BR.   BR.

SECOND FLOOR

BR.

D.R.   KIT.

L.R.

GALLERY

UTIL.   FAMILY

FIRST FLOOR   5

GARAGE

This 90- by 120-foot lot in a suburb of Vancouver is bounded by a street to the north, existing houses to the east and west and a pocket of city-owned parkland to the south. Architect Cheng's task was to insert a house for a family of four into the sloping site, disturbing the terrain and its natural growth as little as possible while maintaining the privacy its thick tree cover promised. The exterior photos suggest how successfully the house was positioned and masked by existing trees.

The plan is simple and unforced. The entry and secondary spaces are aligned along the largely closed north side. The principal spaces open to the south—to views of the parkland and to the city skyline beyond. Upstairs, the master bedroom at the east of the house is linked to the western bedrooms by a bridge that overlooks the double-height living room. A large skylight over the bridge balances the light from the large window openings in the living room. The decks extend the house southward toward the view and their 45 degree cutoff reflects the line of sight to neighbors at the west. The quarter turn of the masonry chimney stack diminishes its apparent mass and projects these 45 degree angles into the vertical plane.

The exteriors are finished in 1- by 4-inch resawn cedar boards applied vertically over a conventional platform frame. The same material is used inside for ceilings. The floors are oil-rubbed oak strip and match the exposed laminated beams, window trim and fireplace lintel. Most of the partitions are finished in gypsum board painted white to catch the shifting shadow patterns and brighten the interiors on dark Vancouver days. Artificial lighting includes both adjustable and recessed fixtures, both types located to augment the natural light.

The inherent modesty of the house, its design subtleties and careful detailing notwithstanding, kept costs moderate.

Architect: James K. M. Cheng
  1345 Laburnum Street
  Vancouver, B.C.
Owner: Mr. & Mrs. Stephen Chiu
Engineer:
  A. Robert Taylor (mechanical)
Contractor: Cervenka Construction
Photographer: James K. M. Cheng

Site, views, and materials all determined the design of this house, whose quiet, romantic look contrasts with its dramatic positioning on the 40-degree slope of a hillside in Belvedere, a quasi-island in San Francisco Bay. The site is full of trees—eucalyptus, cypress, toyon, acacia—and the house, designed by the architect for himself and his family, is set among them, downhill from the street to which it connects by bridge and a long flight of steps. It is tied to the site at three places—where the main floor begins, where the lower floor takes off, and near the end of the projecting lower deck. The view from the south and west is spectacular, including Richardson Bay, the Golden Gate Bridge, the town of Sausalito, and the many varieties of trees on this and adjacent properties. The living room and master bedroom open onto a large deck facing south, and the dining room, on the west, has its own small deck for outdoor eating. Children's bedrooms, playroom and crafts room are on the floor below, with a deck and balcony for outdoor activity onto which the bedrooms and playroom open. Later, when the children are gone, the upper floor can function alone. Landscaping is natural, for the most part, but is supplemented by plants and shrubs in pots.

RESIDENCE FOR MR. & MRS. DANIEL B. GALE, Belvedere, California. Architect: *Daniel B. Gale*. Contractors: *Ireland, Robinson & Hadley*.

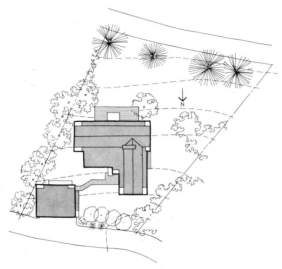

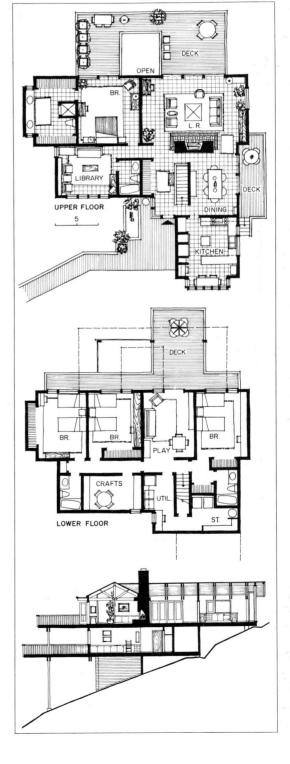

UPPER FLOOR
5

DECK
OPEN
BR.
L.R.
LIBRARY
DECK
DINING
KITCHEN

DECK
BR.
BR.
PLAY
BR.
CRAFTS
UTIL.
ST.
LOWER FLOOR

Merg Ross photos

 Fresh use of traditional materials gives a strong, contemporary character to this comfortable, T-shaped house, which is extremely suitable for the rugged, mountainous terrain of its site in the Colorado countryside

The sense of unaffected ease that is usually evoked by the term "country house," and which has been conspicuously missing from some contemporary houses in rural settings, happily dominates in the design for this home. This is due, in part, to the use of fairly traditional, quiet, textured materials: cedar-shingle siding, columns of stone or exposed aggregate, wood beams, and floors of brick or carpet. And it is also partly due to the simple serenity and sophistication in the handling and combination of the materials. All in all, it is an excellent example of contemporary design that is part of a continuing tradition.

The residence was designed for a couple, both medical doctors, with no children. The site is dry, mountainous terrain covered with prairie grass, which overlooks the city of Denver. According to the architect, the owners required the following, rather typical spaces: "living and dining space for entertaining close friends in limited numbers; a small efficient kitchen with breakfast space; a space for casual entertaining of friends, with a terrace; master bedroom, guest bedroom; study; and enclosed parking."

RESIDENCE FOR DRS. DAVID AND IRMGARD DUBROW, Paradise Hills, Golden, Colorado. Architect: *Donald R. Roark;* structural engineers: *Johnson & Voiland;* electrical engineers: *Sol Flax & Associates;* contractor: *B.B.S., Inc.*

BR.

DEN

UPPER D.R   UPPER L.R

UPPER FLOOR

STUDY

BR.

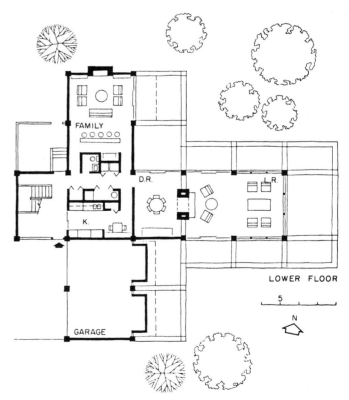

FAMILY

D.R.   L.R.

K.

LOWER FLOOR

5

N

GARAGE

The architect carefully organized the Dubrow's requirements into a cross or "T"-shaped plan, which gives excellent separation for the various living zones. The regular bays of the structure give further definition of some of the spaces.

On the main floor, the stem of the "T" is used for the more formal living and dining spaces in a big, two-story room. The kitchen is the central hub of the plan, flanked by wings for recreation, garages, and a two-story entrance hall. The spaciousness of the main floor is further emphasized by the openness of a balcony-like den on the second level over the kitchen. A master bedroom suite occupies one upper floor wing, the other contains a study and a guest bedroom. The construction cost of the house was $55,345, without lot.

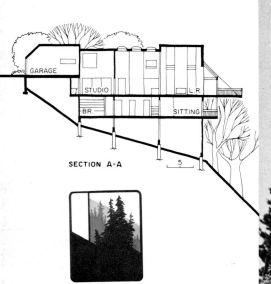

SECTION A-A   5

A steep and picturesque site above the San Francisco Yacht Club on Belvedere Island is the location of architect Rod Friedman's own house. In addition to concern for preserving the stands of oak, eucalyptus and pine on the hillside, he was limited by city ordinance to a two-story scheme. Thus, instead of the compact three- or four-story design one might expect, he has developed a more horizontal concept. Unfortunately, a large volume of enclosed space under the house cannot legally be occupied. Nonetheless, by using an audaciously structured deck and an elegant greenhouse-like solarium, Friedman has made the most of the situation.

The dining room, living room and library, which occupy the most prominent volume of the house (right) are meant to be places where the family gathers and where parties are held. In addition, each family member has his own private space. For the parents, there is a suite on the lower level which includes a sitting room and smaller deck. The wood-framed house is sheathed in vertical re-sawn redwood boards left to weather, a contrast to the white interior walls.

Architect and owner: RODNEY F. FRIEDMAN of Fisher-Friedman Associates. *Location:* Belvedere, California. *Engineers:* L. F. Robinson and Associates (structural); Harding Miller and Associates (foundations). *Contractor:* Clancy Becker.

An adjustable ¾-inch cable on each side of the solarium (above) supports the flying deck. From it (above right), one has a remarkable view of the marina activities. From below, the sailors in turn can compare the structure with the rigging of their boats. The lofty living room (right) and the library beyond are filled with light during the day by skylights and large windows on all sides.

Fisher-Friedman photos

BALCONY LEVEL
455 SQ. FT.

B.R. 2
11x13

BATH

B.R. 3
10x10

DINING
11x14

LIVING
19x23

KIT.
8x11 6

LAUNDRY
8x10

BATH   B.R. 1
13x13

N

FIRST FLOOR
1323 SQ. FT.

Hugh N. Stratford photos

The strong shapes of this compact house closely echoes the site, and affords beautiful views of Lake Sammamish and the Cascade Mountains. As the setting is fairly open, the design of the house organizes solid walls and windows to give privacy from the road, openness to the view. The crisp, angular silhouette of the house is emphasized against the sky by the use of dark brown cedar siding, and copper for flashing and entrance roof.

The interior spaces are arranged on three levels: a raised basement, the main floor, and a partial second floor. The entry which is midway between the basement and main-floor levels, is actually a landing of the open stair constructed of steel and laminated wood. The basement was designed to provide a two-car garage, furnace room, recreation room, study/guest room, bath and darkroom. The top floor contains bedrooms and bath for two sons.

The main floor of the house has a spaciousness not readily apparent from the exterior. The living room is a large one, with a ceiling of suspended cedar paneling that follows the slope of the roof to a maximum height of 14 feet. A window wall and balcony open the space fully to the view. A low-ceilinged dining space is separated from the living area by a freestanding fireplace, yet the rooms are strongly tied together by a floor of red quarry tile—which covers all the main floor except for the carpeted master bedroom. A compact kitchen, with an adjoining laundry room, is placed between the dining area and the entrance stairs for convenience to all parts of the house.

Architect: WENDELL H. LOVETT
Owners: Mr. and Mrs. Peter Meilleur
Location: Bellevue, Washington
Mechanical engineer: Richard Stern
Landscape architects: Richard Haag
  Associates
Contractor: Pacific Northwest
  Construction Co.

The openness of the living-dining and entrance areas of the house is further extended by using a balcony as hallway to the upper-level bedrooms (photo, near right). The structure of the house is wood frame, surfaced with oil-stained red cedar on the exterior, painted plasterboard on the interiors. Aluminum sash is used throughout. Furnace and water heater are both gas fired. The master bath is compartmented, and its counter is tiled in Venetian glass.

Christian Staub photos

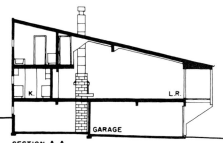

SECTION A-A

This remarkable house near Vancouver, British Columbia, is an affirmation that men can build without violating the natural contexts around them. The property must have long seemed hostile to any construction; it drops forty feet in elevation, through a series of cliffs and foliage areas, to a rock shelf overlooking the Pacific. Yet both the owner, and particularly the architect, Arthur Erickson, recognized the possibilities and the appropriateness of this site for a home. In the sketch shown above, done when the site was still only rocks and trees, Erickson first captured the essence of the house he hoped to create, and it bears a striking affinity to the finished design. The rocks and the vertical pines are of course there in the sketch, but also present are the series of hovering horizontal planes (which has remained the organizing principle of the composition), the cantilevered beams, and even the vertical massing of the stair tower and the masonry fireplace. Erickson's conception provided a logical and encompassing format for his subsequent achievement: a significant example of residential architecture.

HOUSE FOR MR. AND MRS. DAVID GRAHAM, West Vancouver, British Columbia. Architects: *Erickson/Massey*—designer and partner-in-charge: *Arthur Erickson;* job captain: *Garry C. A. Hanson;* landscape: *Erickson/Massey,* contractor: *Sjogren Construction Co.*

The Graham house is insistently horizontal, rectilinear, and rather polished in contrast to the verticals, the random diagonals and roughness of the landscape. Within this fabric, the house at first seems complicated, yet there is an immediately apparent visual organization to it. Simply stated, the house is composed of a series of horizontal terraces stacked along a jagged slope. The terraces, rather than being carved out of the land, were created and expressed by the horizontal box beams which surround each floor. These wooden rectangles seem to jut out from the sloping rock, floating above each other to create the exterior and interior space. The box beams are clearly articulated from the walls and glass which they support. The points of transition between walls and beam are kept absolutely horizontal, and the walls are either glass or strongly textured cedar board and batten, which contrast with the smooth surface of the beams themselves.

The principal material of the house is cedar, with a simple oiled finish which expresses both the color and texture of the wood. Accent materials are an earthen-colored used brick and a dark quarry tile. It is through materials and color that the house seems to join with the site producing a balance with nature and an ordered setting for daily life.

The structural concept of the Graham residence might at first appear to be based on a series of strong cantilevers, yet there is only one within the house: a small balcony off the master bedroom. The projecting ends of the box beams carry only their own weight, and each terrace of beams is supported at its corners by wood posts which carry through to the ground. The box beams provide horizontal support for the ceilings, floors, and stairs, but structural action does not take place through their total depth: they act also as parapet guard rails at the glass lines and around the outside decks.

The several decks and series of rectangles formed by the box beams are readily apparent when seen from above the approach road to the house (photo below). From the water, one can see most of the rugged site and the mountain which towers behind it. Though the site appears to be far from any urban area, the house is supplied with fresh water from a city main about 150 feet away.

The major interior spaces are the living room and the master bedroom, both with sweeping views of the sea and its islands. The box beams form parapets around these spaces, just as they do on the decks, with broad expanses of glass as the principal enclosures. The bedroom and living room are both well separated from the points of entrance and from the kitchen, guest room and work areas.

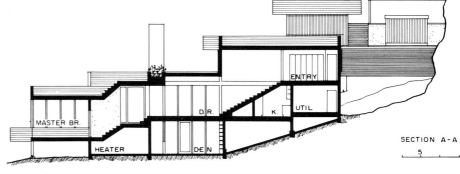

SECTION A-A

A person standing at the entry to the house (above) can see into the guest bedroom and through it to the large terrace over the living room, or he may look down the stairs into the dining room and finally into the living room itself, or he may glance to his left through an entryway window towards the swimming pool, the trees, and the ocean beyond. There is a strong sense of transparency throughout the house, of standing in one room and being able to see through it to several others, yet there is complete privacy from the public eye. The den on the lowest floor, however, provides a feeling of enclosure from the rest of the house, and is the only living space on that floor.

The detailing of these interior surfaces is worth noting. Where sand float plaster is used, there is an integral coloring added, but no paint. Where the floors and ceilings meet the walls, there is always a grooved inset that separates one plane from the other. The recessed down lights and ventilation grilles have specially designed plaster stops; there is no exposed trim piece around them.

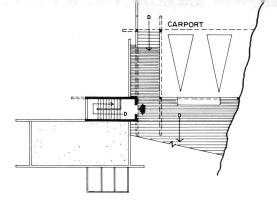

CARPORT & ENTRY LEVEL

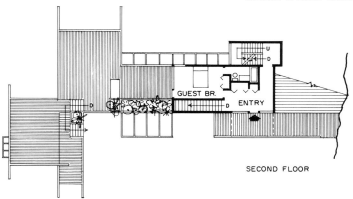

SECOND FLOOR

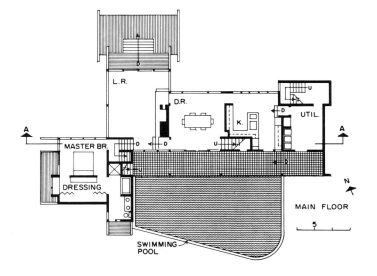

MAIN FLOOR

SWIMMING POOL

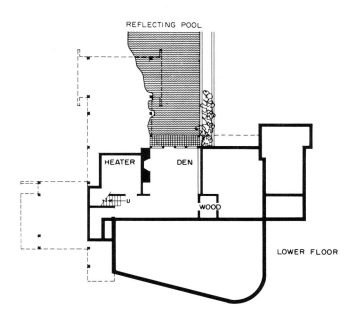

LOWER FLOOR

Approaching by automobile, the visitor first arrives at the carport, at the highest level of the house. The walk from the carport goes down a short series of steps and past a private entrance to the rear stair tower. Guests proceed down a broad outside staircase (pg. 49) to the main entry at the second floor. Once inside the entry, there is a guest room, a bath, and the first of the outside roof decks. A long stair then leads down to the main floor and principal living spaces, including the master bedroom and the swimming pool. In plan, the main floor seems to pinwheel about one of the principal vertical elements of the house, a broad fireplace and chimney stack. Finally, at the lower floor there is storage space, the furnace room and the den, which looks out onto a shallow reflecting pool.

The front third of the house is supported on wood columns set either on isolated concrete piers or anchored directly to the rock (see lower floor plan). Here, foundation and excavation work was minimal and quick. At the rear of the house, however, substantial excavations and trench footings were required, along with retaining walls acting against the slope of the ground.

The owners of this Vancouver house, Mr. and Mrs. Helmut Eppich, came to Canada from their native Germany nearly 15 years ago. They brought with them, as part of a European cultural heritage, a sophistication about architecture and a deeply-ingrained appreciation for fine craftsmanship. Both of these qualities are visibly present in the house architect Arthur Erickson designed for them on this sloping site outside the city.

When the Eppichs purchased the property, which bordered on a small stream, certain problems were apparent. The city had an easement that cut diagonally across the lot near its center. It was a dark lot, much of it shaded by heavy tree cover. Finally, the site had been used as a refuse dump.

Erickson decided to reserve the worst portion of the site—the dumping area—for building and began by developing the site's other potentials. The stream was diverted to create a small pond. Areas were recontoured. Trees were removed to bring in natural light in a climate that includes a large number of gray winter days.

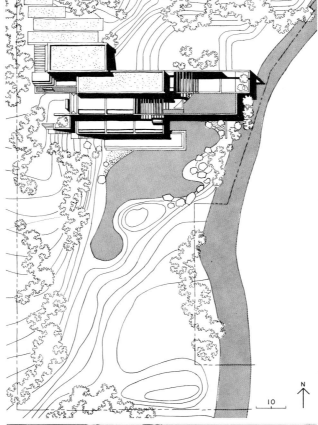

Then, and only then, did Erickson turn to the design of the house. He conceived it as stepping down the contours in a series of transverse elements, the easement being allowed to run through the site between the family room and the pool (see plans). Children's bedrooms were located on the uppermost level, parents' bedroom on the lowest level (not shown in plan). The bulk of the house—living, dining, kitchen, family room—occurs at the intermediate level and shares a large patio.

The Eppich house is ordered and elegant; perhaps more formal in character than other, recent Erickson designs. The craftsmanship and the exceedingly handsome detailing are a tribute to the architect and owner as well as to the builder. They shared a common vision of what was wanted and cooperated to produce it.

Architects: Arthur Erickson/Architects
   Nick Milkovich-project architect
   2412 Laurel Street
   Vancouver, British Columbia
Owners: Mr. and Mrs. Helmut Eppich
Location: Vancouver, British Columbia
Engineers: Bogue Babicki & Associates
   (structural)
   J. D. Kern & Company (mechanical)
Interiors: Francisco Kripacz
Contractors: Stan Burton,
   Deas Construction Co.
Photographer: Simon Scott

The concrete frames of the Eppich house step down the hillside in three evenly graduated bays. This massing not only reduced the apparent height of the house when viewed from across the pond (photo below) but also makes the end elevations (photo left) conform to the general profile of the site.

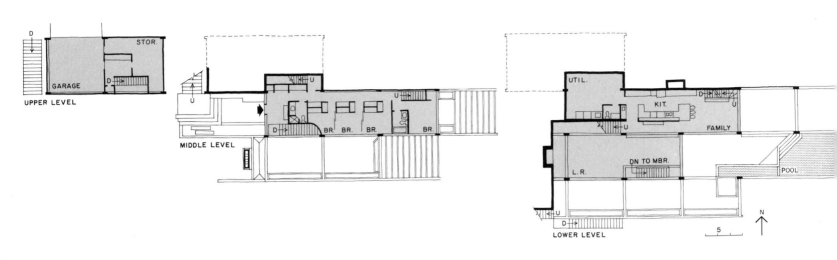

UPPER LEVEL

STOR.

GARAGE

MIDDLE LEVEL

BR. BR. BR. BR.

UTIL.

KIT.

FAMILY

L.R.

DN TO MBR.

POOL

LOWER LEVEL

N

5

The living-dining areas of the Eppich house are located on the intermediate level. In the photo below, the stairs at right lead to the upper-level entry. Stairs at left connect to the den and master bedroom below (photo right). Wood, used sparingly outside, has various interior applications.

This crisp multi-leveled house, relating closely to the slope and character of this small, heavily wooded plot, was designed on a minimum budget by architect Jerry Weisbach. Since the owners wished to preserve the nature of the site while achieving a sense of spaciousness around and within the house, the architect split the house into two rectangular wings and placed them on different ground levels. Consequently, the house is viewed upon approach as a series of broad parallel planes, each of which recedes and descends a bit further into the woods. The result appears quite large, and yet an integral part of the site.

Each of the elements performs a distinct function (see plan below), with the wing nearest the street—containing two bedrooms above the garage—connected to the living wing by a stair tower (shaded in section and plan). The separation of living and sleeping areas into two wings gives the family a great deal of privacy. Privacy was also the factor in shielding the outside balcony off the master bedroom from the street by extending the front wall across it (photo, top right). All other living areas are related directly to the outdoors by large expanses of glass.

A change in ceiling heights throughout the house provides a variety of spatial experiences, variety which is carried into the two-story living room by placing a studio-den on an interior balcony. The interior has been kept in the spirit of the exterior by treating all wall surfaces as simple planes.

The beautifully detailed exterior, clad in redwood siding, reflects the natural surroundings. Left untreated, the redwood will weather with time.

Architect: **Gerald G. Weisbach** of Weisbach/Boutmy/Silver, 55 Stevenson Street San Francisco, California. Owners: *Mr. and Mrs. Medford Schwarz;* engineer: *Fong Chan;* contractor: *A. Von Rotz.*

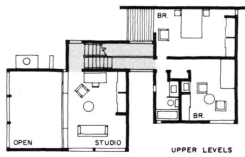

UPPER LEVELS

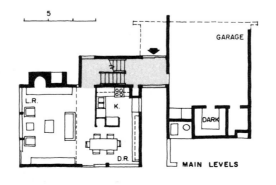

MAIN LEVELS

Built essentially as a series of intersecting planes, this house for a heavily wooded site affords a great deal of privacy for its owners. The various interior levels are designed to closely follow the slope of the site. Extremely controlled detailing gives the design a sense of crispness.

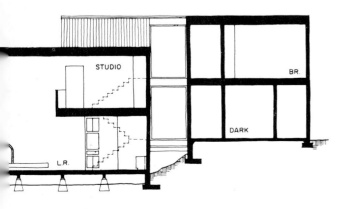

Karel Bauer photos

STUDIO

BR.

DARK

L.R.

SECTION II

HOUSES FOR FLAT SITES

Imaginative design can make up for what a flat site lacks in interest, and the houses on the following pages (in the city, pages 58–90, and in the sub-urbs, pages 91–129) show just how varied the experience of a house on an essentially flat site can be. In many parts of the West, the flat site is no longer available; population pressures have taken care of that. But in other areas, where the land is predomi-nantly flat, the flat site is most common. And in still others, slight changes in level may or may not be used for building on. Examples of various solutions range from the Houston house, which is almost completely closed off from the street (page 60), to the Neutra Research House II (page 86), which achieves its privacy with tall vertical fins of aluminum.

Unlike the hill houses in an earlier section, there is a difference between houses in the city and in the suburbs when their sites are flat. In this selection, at any rate, more formality is noticeably characteristic of the city houses, dictated by the need for a barrier be-tween street and house. Outdoor living is at the rear of the house, with a deck or terrace completely shut off from the street, or in an enclosed court or patio.

The suburban house has a variety of choices,

but privacy is still a consideration. Although the siting of the houses shown here suggests very spacious lots, it is the careful use of the land that creates this sense of space.

IN THE CITY

This elegant, unusually spacious little town house, designed by architect Robert Sobel for himself and his wife, heralds the completion of a remarkable block of privately built, custom-designed houses. Conceived of and started by another Houston architect, Preston Bolton, over a decade ago, the block has been brought to fruition by a strong act of will by all concerned to follow the original ideas. The houses, which line two sides of a private street, are all one story and built of a similar brick—with major exterior variances only in discreet patterns in the brick-work, in the thin roof coping, and in the front doors. The block has a central, communal swimming pool and recreation pavilion; carports and ser-

vice alleys are behind each row of houses. By planning the development as a unit, full use of each lot was possible—with each house gaining light and air from internal courts.

The Sobel house, shown here, possibly has the most open interiors of all the group, being essentially planned as a single room around a garden.

As can be noted in the plan, all principal rooms—entry, living room, dining room and master bedroom—have glass walls flanking the court; even the two study/guest-bedrooms are afforded a corner peek at the foliage. A system of shutters along the living room and bedroom sides of the court provides sun control and privacy

when needed. Unity of all these spaces is emphasized by white plasterboard walls throughout, and by using a single flooring material—a deep purple iron-spot brick—for all rooms, and also for paving in the garden court.

An extra note of spatial drama is added by variations in ceiling heights: most are ten feet, with the entry dropped two feet to emphasize the general spaciousness; at the back of the compound, the dining room ceiling unexpectedly rises in a pyramidal form to a six-foot skylight.

SOBEL RESIDENCE, Houston, Texas. Architect and owner: *Robert Sobel.* Engineers: *Krahl and Gaddy* (structural). Contractor: *Orval Burke.*

60

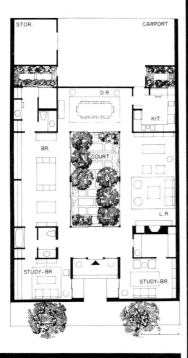

On a 45- by 78-foot buildable lot, architect Sobel has created a house with a great sense of privacy from the outside, and a great flow of space and openness in the interiors. In addition to the central garden court, on which all principal rooms focus, there are little gardens at the entry (right), which also serve the guest bedrooms, and off the master bath and the kitchen (bottom right).

Alexandre Georges photos

To help unify the sense of continuous space in the house, Sobel has used quiet, natural materials for the furnishings throughout: teak, walnut, rosewood, travertine, leather. Bright accents are supplied by rugs and accessories. There are two small studies flanking the entry that double as guest bedrooms (far right). The master bedroom is a luxurious 26 feet long at present (bottom right), but can be divided into two bedrooms in the future.

Economy and privacy were two important design criteria for architect Paul McKim's own townhouse. Built on a small, narrow lot, flanked on both sides by neighboring houses, the residence affords the McKims a good deal of privacy, and a nice sense of the outdoors.

For a house containing 1,600 square feet of living space, the construction cost was unusually low, especially when the beautifully detailed results are considered. Costs were kept to the budget by using a wood-frame, post-and-beam construction with large plaster panels on both the interior and exterior surfaces.

Basically, the design consists of two rectangular wings linked by a stairwell (see plan below). The two courtyards, formed between the wings, give the desired outdoor space and privacy.

The house is zoned so that the children use the left wing and the parents the right. This means of zoning seems to be a good answer to maintaining a level of privacy suitable to both parents and children. The children's bedrooms were placed over the "work" area, which could double as a play room in bad weather.

The interior is enlivened by opening up of the one-story space in the dining area to two-story spaces on both sides—in the living room, and in part of the kitchen.

An especially nice attention to detail is evident in this house. Everything—from the trellis which spans the front courtyard and casts strong shadows down the white plaster wall (see photo right), to the hooded balcony over the garage—achieves the greatest effect by the simplest means. Even the white walls of the courtyard serve the secondary purpose of reflecting the sun into the north side of the living room.

Architect: Paul W. McKim, 3611 Fifth Avenue, San Diego, California. Owners: *Mr. and Mrs. Paul W. McKim;* landscape architect: *Wimmer & Yamada;* interior designer: *Dixon Morrow Jr.;* contractor; *John Worobec.*

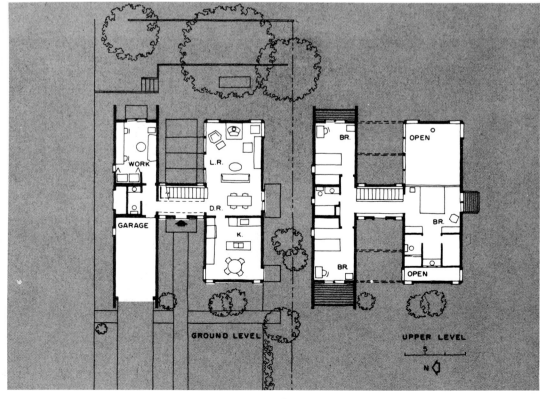

GROUND LEVEL   UPPER LEVEL

An extremely important factor in this architect's own townhouse was the low budget within which he achieved striking spaces, including the two-story living room and a variety of outdoor areas as well.

THIRD FLOOR

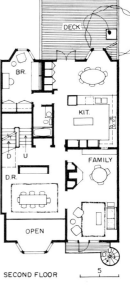

SECOND FLOOR

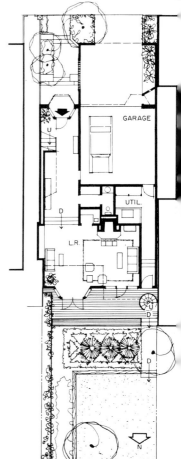

FIRST FLOOR

Jeremiah O. Bragstad photos

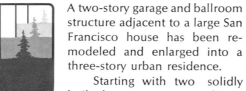

A two-story garage and ballroom structure adjacent to a large San Francisco house has been remodeled and enlarged into a three-story urban residence.

Starting with two solidly built clear span spaces, architect John Field has reworked the structure to allow addition of another floor and has opened the north elevation (above) to the dramatic views of San Francisco Bay. The large bay window, serving living room, dining room and master bedroom on respective floors, is echoed on the street facade by smaller bays (opposite above).

Great care was taken to relate interior spaces to each other, to the views and to the sun. Because the rear play yard seldom receives sun, a south-facing second-floor deck above the driveway was added. On the third floor, a tiny open court catches sunlight for the interior bedroom. Cedar shingles tie old and new parts of the building together and the new house to the old one.

Architect: JOHN LOUIS FIELD of Bull Field Volkmann Stockwell partner-in-charge. *Owners:* Mr. and Mrs. Murray Waldman. *Location:* San Francisco. *Engineers:* Pregnoff, Matheu, Kallam, Beebe (structural); O'Kelly & Schoenlank (mechanical). *Landscape architect:* Thomas D. Church. *Contractor:* Lester Lipinski.

The kitchen-breakfast room, (above) and entry (left) face south, but the most dramatic space in the house faces north toward the Bay. The splendid two-story bay window (right) is part of the new construction added to permit four bedrooms on the top floor. The living-room floor was lowered to grade (below) to allow maximum ceiling height and a new parquet floor installed.

 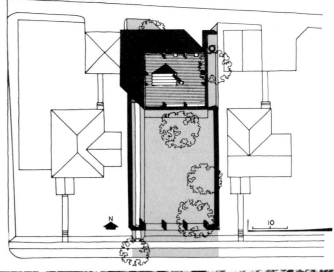

Jonathan King

In designing a house for his own family of four, in a Houston subdivision, architect William Cannady began with two important design decisions. First, he set the house at the rear of the lot creating in this way one large outdoor area instead of two smaller areas and avoiding the standard shoulder-to-shoulder relationship with neighbors. Second, he placed the house over the garage and developed an inviting roof terrace that provided a second usable outdoor space—this one to be used primarily by parents for cocktails and cookouts. The six-foot side yard restrictions and the pattern of existing trees combined to determine the precise siting as well as the 33- by 37-foot outside dimensions.

Kitchen, study, dining and living room, share the second floor and flow easily around a sharply defined central core. The level above is compartmentalized into parents' and children's bedrooms and baths. The floor of the master bedroom is cut back to create a narrow vertical connection with the living room below (section and photo, opposite page).

The structure is standard wood frame, clad inside and out with 1- by 6-inch rough-sawn cedar siding. Painted sheetrock is used selectively on ceilings and third-floor partitions. The floor of the living room level is finished in clay tile imported from Mexico and the roof terrace is 1- by 4-inch redwood decking constructed in pallets.

The budget for this simply constructed but appealing house was small. According to Cannady, this very low cost was achieved for several reasons. The quantity and cost of finish materials was not excessive. But beyond that, almost no unusual detailing conditions were allowed to creep into the drawings and the contractor understood, and was sympathetic to, the architect/owners's rather straightforward design intention from the outset.

Architect and owner: WILLIAM T. CANNADY. Location: Houston, Texas. Engineers: Krahl & Gaddy (structural). Landscape architect: Carlisle Becker. Contractor: Design Fabricators, Gene Hopkins, partner-in-charge.

The creation of a rooftop terrace brought the usable outdoor coverage to virtually 100 per cent of the site—an objective that seems especially sensible for a small lot in a warm climate. Projecting vents are carefully located to intrude as little as possible (photo left). A solid parapet and surrounding trees help to preserve a pleasant sense of privacy when the roof deck is in use.

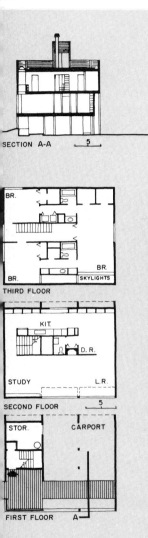

SECTION A-A   5

BR.

THIRD FLOOR   BR.   BR.   SKYLIGHTS

KIT   D.R.

STUDY   L.R.

SECOND FLOOR   5

STOR.   CARPORT

FIRST FLOOR   A

Photos by Richard Payne except as noted

Axial views with their framed vistas are used as a design motif throughout and provide a sense of depth to the compact volume of the house. This spatial design, a classical device illustrated in the photos of gallery, dining and living rooms below, reveals the rich contrasts that make walking—as well as looking—through the house a pleasurable experience, and at the same time reflects the orderly and practical arrangement of its functions.

Creating space and privacy for a restricted city site is a pressing problem graciously met in this trim and elegant home for a family of five. The very personal environment is quite removed from the busy city scene, but imparts a quality of sophisticated precision that reflects urban character at its best. Since the owners already owned a ski house in the Colorado mountains, it was their wish that the Denver townhouse be, in contrast, suited to a formal city style, and at the same time adapted to the varied entertainment requirements of an active social and civic life. The small, flat city lot, removed from the street, suggested the house's compact, two-story scheme. Community and privacy are both assured by basic zoning of the plan—adult activities to the front, with formal areas below and private above, and children's areas and utilities to the rear. All are connected along an organizing central axis, and pivot on a central skylighted spiral stair. Dining and living rooms, gallery and library knit into this axis and can be closed off as formal rooms or fused together for open-house use. A skylighted entrance gallery helps to articulate the upstairs plan while providing a focal point for rooms below. Special elements—including a guest suite and basement sauna—are also neatly incorporated.

RESIDENCE FOR MR. AND MRS. WILLIAM V. WARREN, JR., Denver. Architect: *Carl Groos, Jr.*—*Mardi B. Groos*, associate; structural engineer: *B. W. Lorance*; mechanical engineer: *John Blank.*

Marc Neuhof photos

Facades of the Warren house reflect the owners' request for open, but restrained formality. Glazed areas on three sides are ample, but never aggressive, and are subordinated to the symmetrical scheme. Warm beige brick, imported from Mexico, contrasts with the crisp lines of dark wood sash. The same carefully integrated precision of parts and good materials is carried throughout the interior. Brick and highly polished granite are used in the cool, formal gallery (photo below), and contrast with the rich wood parquet floors of the living areas beyond. Polished beige flagstone over concrete is used for kitchen and baths. The owners collect fine antiques, and both these more ornate pieces and the simpler contemporary furniture are complemented by the timeless quality of both materials and design. The entrance gallery shown below, with its bridge linking upstairs master suite and children's quarters, combines spatial formality and inventiveness in a counterpoint that keynotes the house's design.

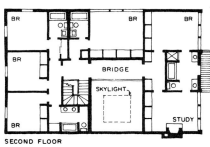

A good site can be a great asset in designing a house and, like a restricted budget, a challenge as well. In this case, the site is a small but a very romantic and private one in Berkeley, California—a wooded lot on the slope of a creek, accessible only by a long bridge. Instead of blending the structure with the woods, architect Donald Olsen has offset—and enhanced—the setting with an uncluttered geometry, equally uncluttered spaces, and a sophisticated choice and handling of major exterior materials: stucco, glass and black aluminum trim. Elegant detailing and expansive spaces were achieved not only within the discipline of simple wood framing and an unusually practical plan, but within a budget of surprisingly small dimensions. Deliberately varied living areas are as strikingly responsive to the potential of the site as the deliberately simple forms; view of the glass-walled living "pavilion" are shown on the following page.

RUTH HOUSE, Berkeley, California. Owners: *Mr. and Mrs. Herman D. Ruth;* architect: *Donald E. Olsen;* engineer: *Jack N. Kositsky;* landscape architect: *Peter Walker, Sasaki, Walker & Associates;* contractor: *Charles Mee.*

Rondal Partridge photos

The dining room is part of the living pavilion shown on the preceding page. Floors are oak strip. Black anodized aluminum is used for sliding doors. "It's a house that's comfortable with our modern furniture," said the client, "but I'm sure that if someone moved in with Louis XV it would look just as well." The site is a small division of a 50-year-old estate designed by Frederick Law Olmsted to provide color throughout the year, and care was taken not only to preserve the huge trees but to return the land, which abounds in rhododendrons, camellias and fuchsias, to its early, "natural" state. A virtual umbrella over the house was created through its careful placement among the trees. Because of this measure, no air conditioning was required. The view, below right, is from the living unit through to the entrance hall. Many vistas and changing shadow patterns add visual interest throughout. The entrance hall gives directly onto the rear terrace, right, to facilitate entertaining outdoors. Everywhere possible opportunity is taken to expand the visual space, but there is plenty of opportunity for privacy as well. A penthouse, shown at right, was designed as "an elevated version of a conversation pit" and gets a view past branches of the trees.

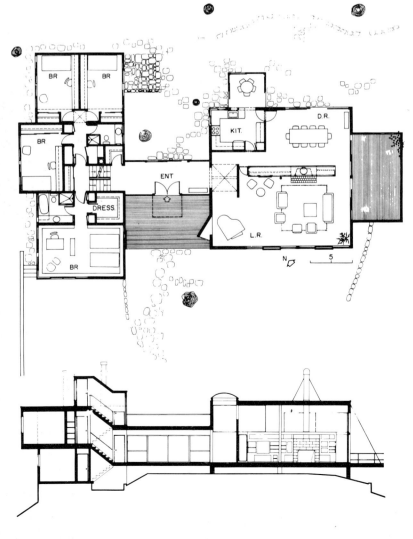

The living pavilion shown on these pages is only 32 feet square but gives the impression of being twice that size. Cabinets, shelves and fireplace are pulled together in a central divider to baffle living and dining areas and leave the perimeter free for glass. Though monochromatic, the house was in fact designed to support bright color, which comes from a yellow rug, red wall tapestry and the large-scale paintings the owners collect.

The family includes three boys, and separation of activities, as well as space for entertaining, was required. Minimal vertical traveling was another major request. Technically, the preservation of the site of several very large oak trees proved the most demanding problem, influencing not only the shape and orientation of the house, but the construction of a foundation made of special shallow-grade beams. A two-unit plan admirably exploits the natural slope and views while meeting practical needs.

In addition to the bedrooms shown in the ground-level plan, the second tighter unit makes use of the slope to dispose a t.v. room on the lower level, with a small, roof-level "penthouse" on the third floor. The owners are delighted with their house. "This house *is* light" they report, and natural light from varied sources does form a major design ingredient, combining with recessed fluorescent lighting and white walls.

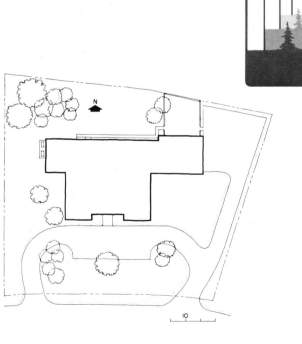

A central "hall" for family visits keys this plan to the needs of the owners, whose children are married and do not live at home, but who wanted the house to provide for visits of their grandchildren. The big room doubles as a foyer, and has a sky-lighted plant area with a central fountain to separate the entry from the family living area. The room opens at back to a covered porch and a terraced back yard. The site is a one-acre lot in a typical Houston subdivision.

The central hall also divides the bed-room areas from the entertaining and service areas of the house. A more formal living-dining room is separated from the hall by screens, which may be opened to join the areas for large gatherings.

Careful planning and the creation of vistas and focal points give this house the appearance—and livability—of a much larger house and a much larger site.

GENITEMPO RESIDENCE, Houston. Owners: *Mr. and Mrs. Joe Genitempo;* engineers: *Cunningham and Lemus;* contractor: *Pelham Construction Co.*

stadt photos

Rick Gardner photos

This gracious south Texas house for a doctor and his wife fills out its trapezoidal site and opens in an irregular "U" to broad views of Galveston Bay. Because the main orientation is toward the west sunscreening for the window walls—particularly those facing the water—was a paramount concern. The simplest, least expensive solution proved to be operable canvas awnings of the store-front variety, a design feature that gently dominates the elevations and gives the house its primary esthetic character. Other design elements are deliberately subordinated. But the simplicity of the elevations is in marked contrast to the complexity of the plan—a complexity that stems in part from the shape of the site, but more, perhaps, from the decision to particularize so many spaces and provide alternate circulation to most.

Because the Galveston region is in the direct path of periodic Gulf Coast hurricanes, architect Howard Barnstone followed the recommendation of the local weather bureau by setting the first-floor elevation at 14 feet above mean sea level, or several feet over natural grade. To take up this differential, Barnstone introduced stairs between the entry hall and the main living areas and he ringed the front and sides of the house with a strip terrace and a flight of redwood steps. The outdoor spaces created by this device are intimately scaled and inviting.

The interiors make generous use of available space. Furnishings are somewhat formal and detailing is straightforward and uncontrived throughout.

Exterior walls of the Levin residence are tempered glass and brick, the floor slab is finished in clay tile, partitions are gypsum board over standard wood stud and ceilings are acoustical plaster. The roof is built-up tar and gravel.

Architect: HOWARD BARNSTONE, *Owners:* Dr. and Mrs. William Levin. *Location:* Galveston, Texas. *Engineers:* Cunningham & Lemus (*structural*); Ralph Speich (*mechanical*). *Interior designer:* Herbert Wells. *Landscape architect:* Ralph Gunn. *Contractor:* Morton Construction Company.

The plan of the Levin house contains several unexpected elements: a master bedroom directly off the living room, a substantial number of internal spaces and secondary circulation between so many spaces. Few of these plan complexities are translated into the massing or into the elevations.

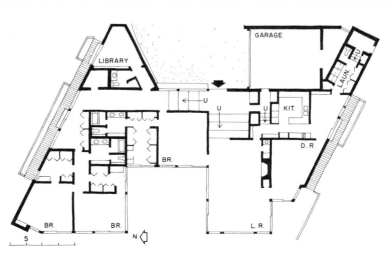

A post-and-beam structure in the California-modern tradition is used skillfully in this spacious house for a small suburban lot in the Santa Monica mountains. The major living areas are oriented with decks and pool to overlook a fine view (photo above). Here, as throughout, architecture, landscape and site combine to offer informal living with a dramatic flair for an active four-member family. The great variety of indoor and outdoor relationships and outlooks has been both created and controlled by skillful structural technique, whose surprising simplicity can be noted above. But the major architectural challenge—all too common a problem, and here, uncommonly well met—was to complete the sizable house within a limited budget—and complete it without skimping on good materials and good craftsmanship essential to this kind of strong, exposed-structure design.

MULLIKIN HOUSE, West Los Angeles, California. Owners: *Mr. and Mrs. Harry Mullikin*, architects: *Dorman/Munselle*; engineer: *Joe Kinoshita*; landscape architects: *Dorman/Munselle*; contractor: *Donald Buhler*.

The outdoors pervades this house, but there is also a great sense of shelter. Living and kitchen areas borrow space from each other and from the outside, and are easily accessible but clearly separated in an open plan. The family room, in foreground of the photo above, has a pass-through counter into a spacious but compact island kitchen. This, as shown in the large photo, opens as well onto the glass-enclosed breakfast alcove, shown also in the photo from the garden, right.

Redwood beams, exposed redwood tongue-and-grooved sheathing, plaster, ans slab floors comprise the materials of the house. Walks are beach-stone aggregate. Cabinets are walnut. Heating is forced air.

The house is well placed on a difficult "flag-shaped" lot, and shares a motor court with another house close by. Thus the entrance side (photos to the left) is screened off and somewhat formal, with large glass areas reserved for southern exposure and outlook to the rear. Small gardens are created behind stucco baffle walls in the front.

A basic "H"-shaped scheme zones bedrooms from activity areas, provides an entry easily accessible to both, and admits light and air throughout. This simple three-part plan suits the structure well, and is effectively framed by it. Exposed beams are handsomely finished, logically placed on a seven-foot module, and always expressive of spatial organization—often dramatically so. Note especially the walkway and entry. In living areas, open planning reinforces glass walls for an over-all flow of space. Freestanding elements—white-brick fireplace and walnut cabinets—interplay with the strongly exposed redwood structural members while effectively zoning functions.

The family includes two teenagers, and since all do frequent entertaining, both space and privacy had to be assured. In the living wing, teenagers can snack and watch television without disturbing (or being disturbed by) parents entertaining in the more formal living area, or the whole wing can work together with outdoor decks and pool for large-scale parties and general family use.

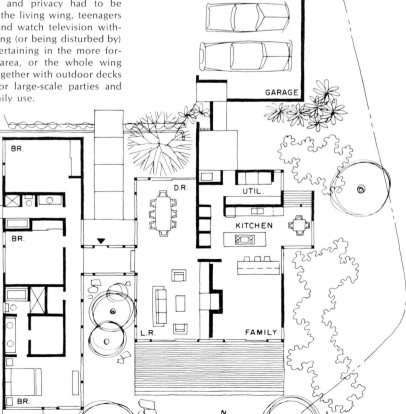

For the design of this Arizona house, architect Judith Chafee retained certain easily recognizable features of the Southwest desert vernacular, but departed from these traditions by the extensive use of window wall and a double band of clerestories on the north elevation. The east elevation is punctured sparingly, with glazing protected from the sun by broad concrete eyebrows. Similar sun-screening devices protect the openings to the south. This combination of openings admits generous amounts of natural light that rebounds off every interior surface but is almost glarefree. A secondary level of glare control is provided by aluminum blinds mounted to concrete lintels over openings in the living room and bedroom.

These interior spaces are loft-like in their arrangement and spatial simplicity and the selection of materials that require little or no finish—block for walls, concrete slab for floor—ensures easy maintenance. The details, like the spaces, have an agreeable simplicity and an unforced regional flavor. The furnishings combine antique and contemporary pieces unself-consciously and reflect the owner's interest in Southwest Indian crafts and artifacts. In siting and landscaping, architect and owner have respected the indigenous flora and, in effect, invited the desert right to the doorstep. The concrete downspouts are a design device taken from a local Spanish mission. Rainwater is conveyed from the roofs down to planters raised off grade to a comfortable working height.

Because the climate is hot and because the house is so open, air conditioning is a practical necessity. Exposed ductwork throughout the house gives forceful expression to this necessity as it penetrates the roof in an appropriately bold visual sweep.

Architect: Judith Chafee
    317 North Court
    Tucson, Arizona
Private residence
near Tucson, Arizona
Contractor: Richard Kesterson
Photographer: Glen Allison

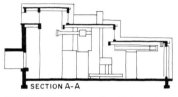

SECTION A-A

In the more usual desert vernacular, small openings puncture heavy masonry walls. The glare that results is troublesome and often throws foreground objects into high-contrast silhouette. By opening the house more generously—particularly overhead—the architect has been able to flood the interiors with daylight and all but eliminate the vexing problem of desert glare.

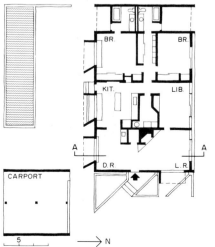

BR.   BR.

KIT.   LIB.

A   A

CARPORT

D.R.   L.R.

5   ⟶ N

When Van der Leeuw Research House I was built in 1932, serving as both office and home for Richard Neutra, its design was primarily intended to demonstrate the application to house design of building methods up to then used on commercial and industrial buildings. But this house provided, above all, a major lesson in how to design for the small urban lot—in this case, 60 by 70 feet—so as to provide privacy and a sense of space for the residents. The design was determined as much by Neutra's philosophy of an architecture, in which human needs and biology make up the major influence, as it was by the new materials—pressed wood; steel sash; large glazed areas and sliding doors; custom-built, fire-enameled metal coverings; and methods, such as prefabricated reinforced concrete joists and sus-

pended arched concrete floor slabs, which were used in it. After a fire in 1963, the house had to be rebuilt, and some changes were made. The exterior was changed by the addition of a glass-enclosed penthouse and vertical aluminum louvers, shaped like jet plane wings and automated to turn with the sun, compensating for the loss of surrounding trees. Some changes were also made in the interior and on the patio side of the house. The lower floor was replanned to serve as headquarters of the Richard Neutra Institute and the upper floor as a private apartment.

Although the rebuilt house shows fewer radical innovations than the original, it represents further exploration of the relationship between human comfort and technology.

VAN DER LEEUW RESEARCH HOUSE II, Los Angeles, California. Architect: Richard J. Neutra; research and project architect: Dion Neutra; structural and civil engineers: Tom Woodward and Stanley Malora; civil engineer: Arthur Levin; mechanical engineers: John Keer Associates; structural engineer: Joseph Kinoshita and Associates; contractor: Walter R. Johnson.

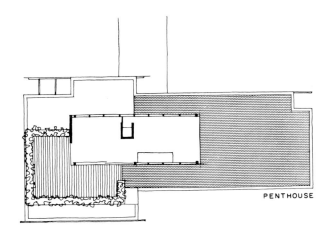

PENTHOUSE

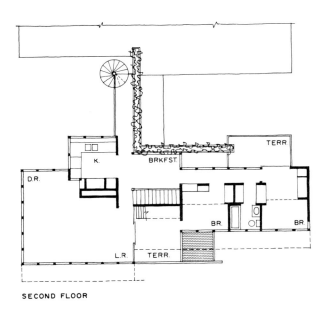

SECOND FLOOR

Jim McCrary

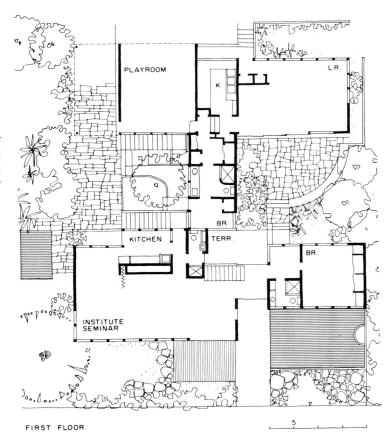

FIRST FLOOR

The roof surrounding the glass-enclosed penthouse is flooded with water which insulates it from the hot California sun (below). More important, a certain ambience is created in which the penthouse becomes a sequestered pergola visually linked to Silverlake beyond. A number of structural innovations were also made, mostly to insure that this second house would not burn. In Research House II, electricity becomes an important element. A new electrical system allows for versatile lighting effects, intercom paging, stereo music, fire-alarm signal and FM-TV antenna distribution throughout the house.

Industrial photo service

Rooms are compactly knit around two patios (above and below) and a spatial unity is achieved between inside and outdoors. A terrace (right below) off the Neutras' bedroom suite is open to the patio below, but is raised above the garden house so as to allow a view of Silverlake to the east. The new penthouse (right middle and above) is a "glazed island." Water retained on the second-story roof gives the illusion of being an extension of the lake's surface.

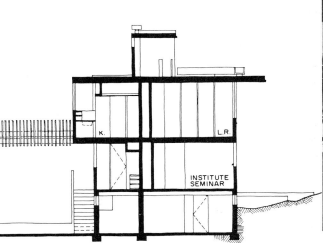

K.   L.R.

INSTITUTE
SEMINAR

5

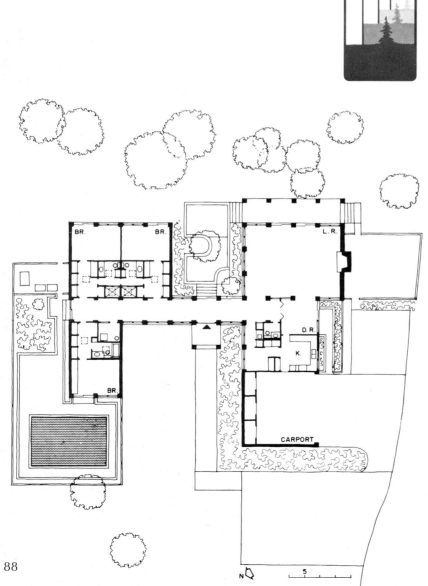

An elegant concept of linked pavilions and colonnades has been developed by Preston Bolton for this fairly large and formal house. It forms a very appropriate scheme for the ample site, and affords desirable views of the large trees and small stream on the property. On the street facade, a generous setback and solid brick walls for major rooms give the needed privacy. A wide entrance gallery, which adds greatly to the sense of style in the house, separates the entertaining areas and the bedroom areas into a bi-nuclear plan. A separate, working artist's studio was placed in a quiet location across the stream, on axis with the house and accessible by a bridge. Champagne-colored Mexican brick is used.

BR.   BR.   L. R.

BR.

D. R.

K.

CARPORT

N   5

Spacious interiors focus on planned vistas through glass walls set between the modular pattern of brick columns. Concrete slab floors have terrazzo or oak finish.

HALPERN RESIDENCE, Houston. Owner: *Leonard Halpern;* engineers: *Cunningham and Lemus;* landscape architect: *Courtade;* contractor: *Alan Huvard Associates.*

The Halpern house affords an excellent example of the architect's concern with indoor-outdoor relationships of spaces for day or night use: Its meticulous detailing and vigorous use of color in all cabinet work (the kitchen doors below are a strong yellow ochre) add vitality to its striking simplicity.

Jerry Bragstadt photos

IN THE
SUBURBS

For some time architects Booth & Nagle have been interested in applying the systems approach to residential design, and the Magnuson house, on Vashon Island, Washington, offered an opportunity for further experiment. The architects began with an 8- by 36-foot core which houses bathrooms, stairs and mechanical spaces. To this core, they added 12- by 12-foot modules that in combination enclose the prime spaces of the house. On the lower floor, two such modules are given over to children's bedrooms, with bunks designed in a stepped arrangement that can accommodate four in each room. The middle level, including living, kitchen and dining areas, is free-flowing and open, although the visible 12-foot framing module provides a gentle spatial definition. The upper level is a master bedroom suite that includes an 8- by 12-foot study that forms part of the core. On middle and upper levels, deck space is added by bridging between modules and thereby eliminating the need for additional footings and columns. At grade, a pleasant outdoor space is created under these projecting decks (photo right). Major window openings are large in response to good views and a cool, damp climate with a high proportion of overcast days.

The Magnuson house sits securely on a narrow plateau on this otherwise sloping site. The architects were careful to preserve both the contours and the natural vegetation. Only one tree was sacrificed during construction.

The Magnuson house, though largely built on the site, was relatively inexpensive to construct. In its careful dimensioning and modular conception, it anticipates houses designed by the architects and now in project form, that will be factory-built and assembled on the site from large prefabricated components.

Architects: Booth & Nagle, Ltd.
   230 East Ohio Street
   Chicago, Illinois
Owner: The Reverend and
   Mrs. George Magnuson
Location: Vashon Island, Washington
Engineers: Raymond Beebe (structural)
Contractor: Philip A. Gregersen
Photographer: Christian Staub

UPPER LEVEL

MIDDLE LEVEL

LOWER LEVEL

The massing of the Magnuson house changes substantially from elevation to elevation but its box-like character remains. The consistent use of window wall as a counterpoint to diagonal siding gives the exteriors a welcome unity—a unity that carries through to the interiors where these same materials predominate and are echoed in the diagonal pattern of the strip maple flooring.

The main approach and entry are from the uphill side across a wood bridge (photo above). The visitor arrives at the intermediate level that includes living, dining and kitchen spaces.

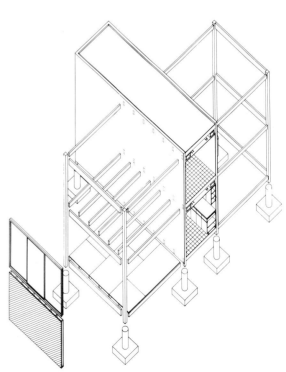

The diagram above establishes the framing principles, indicates mechanical installations, and shows the panel construction.

Richard Payne photos

A limestone arroyo outside Austin, Texas is the site for this exceptional house by Atlanta architect Robert Nichols. The owners, Mr. and Mrs. J. Hiram Moore, are a semi-retired couple who entertain frequently and require a house generous enough in scale to accommodate large numbers of guests. Both owners and architect wanted the house to respond to the unique features of the site and, as a result, the stream bed was dammed to form ponds and the heavily wooded walls of the arroyo were left untouched. The house reaches across, carried where necessary on point supports, to touch each edge and embraces two large trees carefully preserved to form the focus of small interior courts (see plan). The

rooms develop in strict rectangular volumes around these courts. The west elevation facing the entry is mostly solid for privacy and sun control while the house opens around the interior courts and eastward toward the water course. As a result of the siting and massing, the Moore house is almost invisible from surrounding roads.

The house, framed in wood and steel, seems to float effortlessly over its site—a visual effect achieved in part, at least, by substantial cantilevers. Redwood siding, put up in both horizontal and diagonal patterns, covers the exterior. Interior walls and ceilings are finished in drywall or oiled red cedar. All counters, bathroom walls and the kitchen are covered in bright-colored plas-

tic laminate selected to contrast with the cedar. All windows are actually sliding door assemblies framed in anodized aluminum; when open, the windows add the space of the surrounding decks—as well as that of the interior courts—to the living space in the house.

In addition to its imaginative siting and its clear sense of order, the Moore house is exquisitely detailed and constructed, the result of a level of design scrutiny where almost nothing is left to chance.

J. HIRAM MOORE RESIDENCE, Austin, Texas. Architect: *Robert Nichols*. Engineers: *Carroll Claycamp (structural)*; *William Kellett (mechanical)*. Contractor: *Andrew Patton*.

BR. BR.

PORT

L.R.

KIT.

5

BR

Richard Payne photos

The Moores are especially pleased with their new home, but require more storage space than the program originally anticipated. One of the small interior courts may therefore be partially enclosed—an alteration that will effectively enlarge the dining area as it produces additional space for storage.

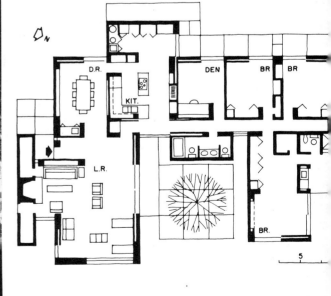

The design of this house began with some deed restrictions—which (in addition to the requirement that the fence, if any, be three-rail, white) called for a shingle roof and white walls. Within this arbitrary discipline, architect Gibbs—for his own house—set his own discipline: an extraordinary effort to, in his own words, "design away the detail." And this effort has indeed established the character of the house. There is, for example, no trim inside or out—fixed glass panels are slip glazed into the plaster or ceiling recesses, and the glass doors (which ride in specially shaped head and sill tracks) slide into pockets built into the walls (see plans). The interior doors have no jambs, heads, or sills—but pivot on floor and ceiling and are stopped by half-inch changes in the wall plane.

This attention to detail

Wayne Thom photos

On the exterior, the rough shingle roof, the unadorned plaster walls, and the glass openings are all treated in a manner that is thoroughly contemporary, but fits comfortably in a conservative neighborhood. Inside, the same sense of big planes of material exists—but all is warmed by the light and the views, and the strongly contrasting framework of ceiling and floor. The kitchen, upper right, was designed to be a "living place, not just a work place,"—it is carpeted, with teak cabinets and work tops. And everywhere, the 10-foot-high ceilings add a sense of space and dramatize the painstaking attention to detail.

fits into a most disciplined basic concept: a dark ceiling plane (stained redwood) and a dark floor plane (wool carpet) that provide limits for the strong white element of the plaster walls. Says Gibbs: "A conscious attempt was made to resolve the walls into many clean rectangular planes and forms—and furnishings, people and plants look well against them."

The house is framed in wood—and the details "respect the notion that it is either expensive or impossible to get finished wood joinery or detail work in the field." The plan offers the downhill views of the city and ocean to the living room, the master bedroom, and to the courtyard framed by these rooms. But all rooms—by use of the panels of glass and screening—can be as open (or as closed) as the family wishes, to the yard, the breeze and the outdoors.

Architects: DONALD GIBBS & HUGH GIBBS
3575 Long Beach Boulevard, Long Beach, California
Owners: Mr. & Mrs. Donald Gibbs
Location: Palos Verdes Peninsula, California
Landscape architect: Bettler Baldwin
Interior design: Donald Gibbs
Contractor: Lyman Merril

The Lauren Studebaker House, winner of the Seattle Times "Home of the Year" award, is located in a deciduous forest setting on Mercer Island, Washington. Three distinctive red cedar-clad forms dominate the uneven terrain. They consist of two hard-edged angular volumes penetrated playfully by expanses of glass and a third, the cylindrical skylit stairwell.

According to Wendell Lovett, its architect, the house was planned "for varying activities and moods of a young family of five." This was accomplished

with great sensitivity by relating the internal functions to various solar exposures. Southerly oriented rooms are generally for active pursuits while the northern spaces tend to be quiet and individualized. A dynamic visual enrichment is exploited with vistas of the east and south channel of Lake Washington which vary with the season.

Further zoning which adds to the spatial variety occurs vertically on three levels: communal and family activities located on mid- or entry-level; children's rooms expressed in a day-

light basement with playrooms opening onto a terrace; and adult sleeping located on the top level for maximum privacy.

The warm character of the natural materials used outside is carried inside as a reflection of a totally enveloping experience.

Architect: WENDELL H. LOVETT. *Owners:* Mr. and Mrs. Lauren Studebaker. *Location:* Mercer Island, Washington. *Engineer:* Richard Stern (mechanical). *Landscape architects:* Sakuma/James. *Contractor:* S. G. Moshier and Sons.

UPPER LEVEL

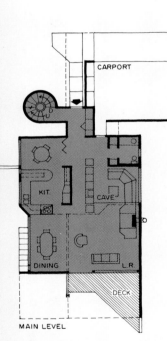

MAIN LEVEL

5   ▷N

LOWER LEVEL

Christian Staub photos

The projecting fireplace is clearly the focal point of the Studebaker house. On one side is the enclosed and cozy center for family activities, nicknamed the "cave" by the architect. On the other is the spacious and open living-dining room. The cave is enlivened by a handsome activity wall containing audio-visual equipment. The breakfast room and kitchen (above) are equally well detailed with the same lively character. The living-dining room, on the other hand, relies on a soaring wood ceiling and natural vistas for a more serene atmosphere.

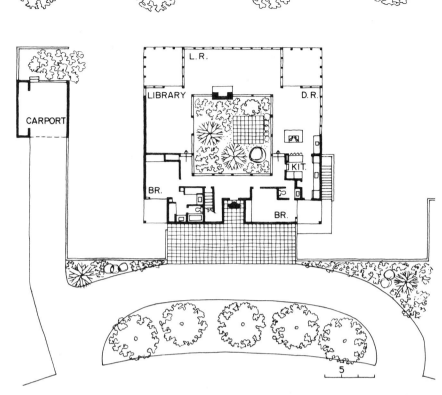

This house, planned around an interior garden covered by a 24-foot-square skylight, is designed to compensate for Colorado's arid climate. The result is the creation of a special environment "where vines rather than walls are used to separate living areas," as the architect describes it. The rapid rate of plant growth in the garden was a surprise: within a year, many kinds of ferns and evergreens, grapefruit, lemon and banana trees were thriving, and poinsettias were nine feet tall.

In a further effort to counteract the semibarren countryside, there are several enclosed exterior spaces. The fencing around the greater part of the property is of cedar plywood with redwood battens, to match the exterior wood surface of the house and make it an integral part of the front façade.

The main living, kitchen and bedroom areas are disposed around the garden on the ground floor, but a balcony over the kitchen and bedroom areas provides two additional bedrooms, a bathroom and a study for the two teen-age children. A partial basement is included beneath the kitchen-dining room area.

The closed-in front or street façade is in sharp contrast to the back of the house where glass walls open to a view of an adjacent golf course to the south and west, with the Rocky Mountains in the background. The deep, sheltering roof provides physical and psychological protection in a climate of extremes.

Architect and owner: Hobart D. Wagener. *Location:* Boulder, Colorado. *Structural engineer:* W. B. Johnson; *Contractor:* R. C. Grayson Construction Company.

Norman McGrath photos

The roof structure is as dramatic a feature of the interior of the house as it is of the exterior. The simple, symmetrical composition of laminated wood beams and cedar decking is complemented by the wire-glass skylight area and the glass walls on the southern and western exposures.

The kitchen is divided into two areas, which can be separated by means of an oak folding door. In this way, the messy area can be closed off during meal-times, leaving the diners with a view of the rather attractive free-standing range and, as Hobart Wagener puts it, "the visually interesting part of food preparation."

The garden, which naturally enough is the main focus of the living areas, has its own central focus in the form of a brick island which makes an excellent base for sculpture, pottery or any kind of garden feature. A stone slab path leads through the garden to the island.

Furnishings are deliberately simple and elegant to avoid any conflict with the strongly articulated structure and plan of the building.

Gas-fired, forced-air heating and refrigerated cooling make for a comfortable environment at all seasons of the year.

In this California house for an artist, architect Thornton Abell was asked to a place a dual-use residence/studio on a site which contained excellent trees and shrubbery. Its dual-use meant that circulation patterns must be clear, and that privacy for the residence must be consciously maintained. The trees and vista seemed to demand that the architecture reach out to the land. Within these parameters, Abell has created a gracious and simple design, epitomized in the elegance of its central court (below). With the character of its foliage, the entrance area seems to encompass a piece of the site, rather than be a man-made court. Yet it is a court which not only provides a circulation focus for the plan, but remains a rather private place within the house and its site.

Julius Shulman photos

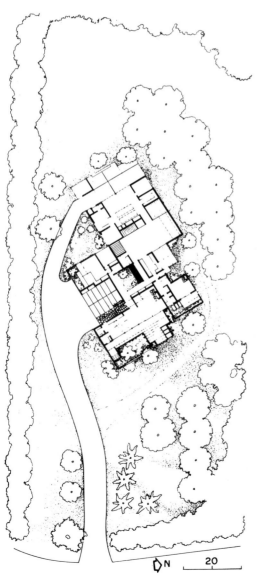

N 20

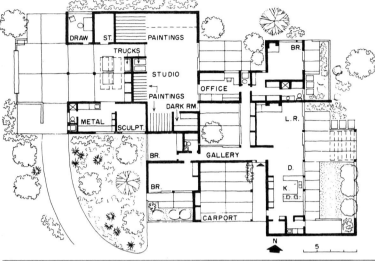

The grounds comprise over an acre in a wide canyon, with the access road to the east screened by a natural drop in the land and heavy planting on a knoll between road and house. Part of the site was covered by an orchard of fruit trees, and the house was carefully located to save them. Excellent foliage helped dictate the choice and character of the material. Plain board-formed concrete has been used throughout the house, on both the interior and exterior. It is a simple, strong surface which creates a backdrop for the closely planted shrubbery and reflects well the intricate shadows cast upon it. As with all exposed concrete, quality workmanship is essential; these walls reflect the conscientiousness of the contractor as well as the skill of the architect. The walls repeat so well the boards that formed them that, in the living room and bedrooms, it is difficult to distinguish texturally between concrete wall and wooden floor.

In addition to the interior court at the entrance, there are four exterior courts enclosed by low-walled extensions from the house. Instead of these walled planting areas being "the outside coming in," they seem to extend the house past its heated and air-conditioned boundaries, as if it were reaching out, and about to grow further. Details such as these add spaciousness to what is basically a small residence and professional studio, each well separated but immediately accessible to the other.

HOUSE IN MALIBU, California. Architect: *Thornton M. Abell;* contractor: *H. P. Marks and Sons.*

The owner required, in addition to living, sleeping, and cooking areas, a flexible studio for the painting and storage of large canvases, provision for sculpturing in metal and plaster, a photographic dark room, and an office area. The studio has extensive storage and supply spaces and a loading area accessible to trucks. As in the living areas, board-formed concrete is used throughout the studio, with the addition of some framed cabinet work and exposed wood. The continuous skylight at the rear of the studio adds dramatic lighting. Studio and office have their own semi-enclosed court, bounded on the east by the chimney and the concrete wall of the master bedroom.

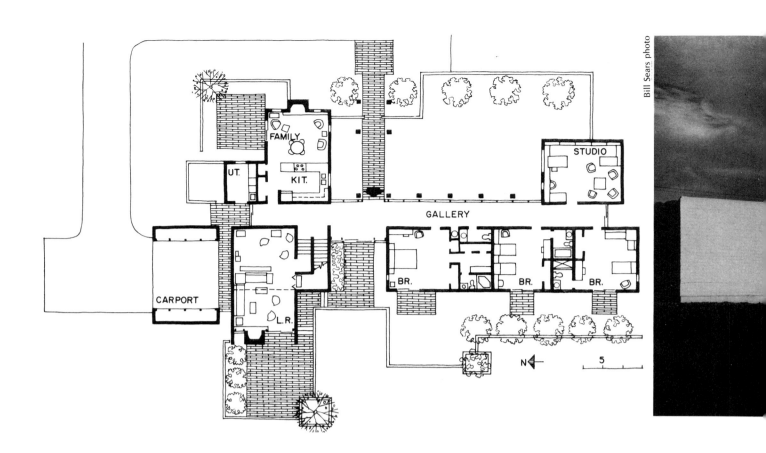

Bill Sears photo

FAMILY

UT.

KIT.

STUDIO

CARPORT

L.R.

GALLERY

BR.

BR.

BR.

N

5

At first glance, this is a very regional Arizona house; but much more important is its expression of the universality and adaptability of some of the current contemporary-design idioms. Shed roofs, a relatively loose (but well-zoned) room arrangement, variety in ceiling heights and levels, a "tumbled" (but carefully studied) interplay of exterior forms, and experimentation with light, shade, shadows and views, are all design devices which are being employed in many of the newer houses from Maine to California. The singularly local quality that they project in this house stems mainly from the use of adobe-like, mortar-washed concrete block (instead of the wood plank, cedar shingles or brick of other regions), and the desert flora.

It is a quite sophisticated, contemporary house, with privacy and space well organized for a family of four. And, over-all, the design has considerable sensitivity and verve—with one small lapse at the entrance, where some columns and panel doors salvaged from several razed buildings have been added, and which are rather out of scale and character with the freshness of the design. It is certainly one of the more interesting of the newer houses in Arizona.

In planning the house for his own family, Bennie Gonzales comments that, "materials and the form of construction were chosen for their suitability to local climatic and cultural aspects. A variety of pleasant, comfortable spaces are provided throughout the house. And it fulfills Gonzales' own program quite well: "Because this residence had to provide privacy for both small and large groups, the rooms are isolated so that various activities need not interfere with each other. The separate portions of the house are clustered as if independent units of a self-sufficient nature. The more or less public areas are comprised of the two-level living area (with a dining mezzanine serviced by a dumbwaiter); a study which can serve for conferences with architectural clients; and a generous gallery, which serves both as hallway and as a spacious area for large numbers of guests in 'party conversation' or at small tables for luncheon. The bedrooms are self-contained, and have sliding glass doors offering a generous view of the desert over an expanse of green. The kitchen is a sort of keeping room, and is spacious enough for leisurely breakfast or lunch."

Architect and owner: Bennie M. Gonzales. *Location:* Phoenix, Arizona. *Engineer:* William Meier. *Consultant:* Richard Joachim. *Contractor:* Frank Gonzales.

This very successful example of a house designed within the disciplines of built-for-sale construction techniques was designed by Claude Oakland for California builder Joseph Eichler. It offers excellent quality and great flexibility within a very low budget.

The builder's program called for a house that could adapt easily to many styles of informal living, and still maintain an intimacy and privacy for its future owners.

The house opens to the rear onto a fenced-in terrace. On the sides exposed to neighbors and the street, glass is kept to a minimum, and the house looks instead upon an atrium at its center. The floor plan is quite open so that a sense of informality works throughout the interior. The warm California climate allowed the use of many glass areas which relate all the areas.

This house is a variation on the popular plan that articulates functions around a central atrium. While the plan is designed for easy circulation, the living and dining areas are defined by the low brick wall and three-quarter-height chimney between them. In the dining area the ceiling is low and flat, and opens to a high gable roof over the living room. Of the four bedrooms, one was placed next to the atrium so that it could double as a library or a family room if the need arises. The kitchen was placed near the garage to cut grocery lugging.

Open gables forming clerestory windows increase the great feeling of spaciousness provided by an exposed post-and-beam structure. Detailing has the virtue of simplicity and control.

All houses in the development have high-pitched roofs and the size and shape of these forms vary to give the community both variety and unity. The twin roofs lend a trim and sprightly character.

Architects: Claude Oakland & Associates, 111 New Montgomery Street, San Francisco. Owner and contractor: *J. L. Eichler Associates, Inc.;* engineers: *Richard J. Huyck & Associates; Robert Ritter (heating).*

Designed as part of a development community, this house is far more than the usual built-for-sale house. Since most people who buy such houses have children, one design imperative was the use of rugged materials which will stand up to youthful abuse. Also, since most younger parents do some entertaining, the house is kept open for a feeling of spaciousness. Yet when there are not crowds in it, sensitive detailing of all the materials lend a feeling of warmth and intimacy.

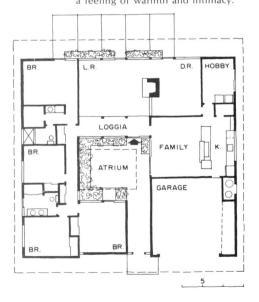

Joshua Freiwald photos

Rush McCoy photos

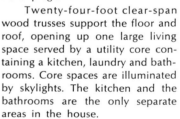

A tight budget and an open-space program determined the design of this house built by Theodore Grossman for his wife and himself. The Miesian idiom, now more the exception in the design of houses than the near-rule it once was, met both the economic and the spatial requirements of the Grossmans' program.

Twenty-four-foot clear-span wood trusses support the floor and roof, opening up one large living space served by a utility core containing a kitchen, laundry and bathrooms. Core spaces are illuminated by skylights. The kitchen and the bathrooms are the only separate areas in the house.

The house is located among pine trees and small rolling hills just east of the front range of the Rocky Mountains. Interior space is intended to relate to this natural setting and also provide a setting itself for objects and art works which the owners collected while they served as Peace Corps Volunteers in Colombia.

Sliding windows on the long sides are glass infill, permitting expression of the structural piers (all structure is wood); solid end-walls emphasize the direction of the trussed rafters.

Warm colors and materials soften the somewhat severe lines of the house. Siding is light-stained plywood with plank finish (left). Exterior decking is redwood; interior floor in the living space is oak. The front door is bright sky blue. Furnishings emphasize reds, whites, yellows, and black.

Architect and Owner: THEODORE A. GROSSMAN, JR., the TAG Associates 975 Grant Street, Denver, Colorado
Location: Parker, Colorado
Contractor: Gerle Bros., Inc.

No doors separate the bedrooms and study from the rest of the interior, above. The wall around the study and large closet, right, does not reach the ceiling but serves as a non-structural screen from the living-dining area.

The odd shape of the lot on which this house is built comes from the creek which meanders along one side; and while it made for some challenging problems, it also provided exceptional advantages of which the architect has availed himself. The house is placed in the most open part of the one-acre lot, where it gets both sunlight and a fine view down the creek, and remains secluded and protected from the road by the splendid grove of redwoods which are on the site. The house angles with the curve of the creek, so that almost every room gains by having a view of the creek. Skylights and clerestory windows not only bring in welcome amounts of sunlight but allow for views into the treetops from rooms otherwise without an outlook. The budget for the house was small, especially in relation to the spaces desired. The result, however, belies any sense of restriction, and as the architect says, "There was never a compromise with finish materials: we used cedar shingles on the exterior, and hardwood floors and handmade tile inside." By opening the main rooms to each other, horizontally and vertically, the interior spaces seem larger than they actually are, an effect enhanced by the amount and quality of the natural light which various types of openings admit, and by the relation of interior spaces to the large deck off the living and dining rooms. The plan is unusually compact, and allows for considerable flexibility in use of the house: some of the open areas can be closed off for privacy and quiet, an apartment over the garage and the future addition of an already-designed family room are other features of this flexibility.

This orderly framing system is based on a four-foot module, with beams exposed throughout the house. The architect/owner was also contractor and, to keep costs down, did much of the construction himself.

Architect: James E. Caldwell, Jr.
  243 Vallejo Street
  San Francisco, California
Owners: Mr. & Mrs. James E. Caldwell, Jr.
Location: Woodside, California
Engineers:
  Shapiro, Okino & Hom (structural)
  George Aronovsky (mechanical)
Interior designer: Philipa Caldwell
Landscape architects: Richard Schardt
  Thomas Church
Contractor: James E. Caldwell, Jr.
Photographer: Philip Molten

SECOND FLOOR

FIRST FLOOR

SECTION A-A

Clerestories, skylights and windows give this house an extraordinarily light and open feeling, and the easy flow of spaces both vertically and horizontally suggests that the house has more than its actual 2,100 square feet of space. Without cramping or crowding, the compact plan has no wasted spaces.

"Overlapping sheds with skylight spaces between forms" is Clovis Heimsath's description of his design concept for this house, which was built in Houston for a sculptor and his family. A strictly limited budget and the requirement for two studios in addition to comfortable family living areas made this a challenging program for the architect. Mr. Heimsath solved the problems by adopting a shed-roof motif which allowed sufficient height and volume for the creation of exciting two-story spaces and constantly changing patterns of light and shade inside and out.

Visual continuity of space between floors was very important since budget restrictions limited floor area, but a "row of little rooms" would have been functionally and esthetically unacceptable to the clients and the architect. The height was emphasized by strategically placed skylights which serve to extend the experience of space.

The first two-story space is the dramatic entry which is spanned by the hall on the second floor; the upstairs studio is a balcony above the sculpture studio on the lower level. The third two-story dimension is provided by the master bedroom which overlooks part of the living room.

The plan was developed around a central core, which consists of washer-dryer facilities and a powder room downstairs, two bathrooms above and necessary ductwork. The architect insists that this is where the scheme started. He says: "The design truly developed from plan to form. The clients had two children and might later add to the family, so the plan had to have three bedrooms, two studios, two and a half baths, living room and

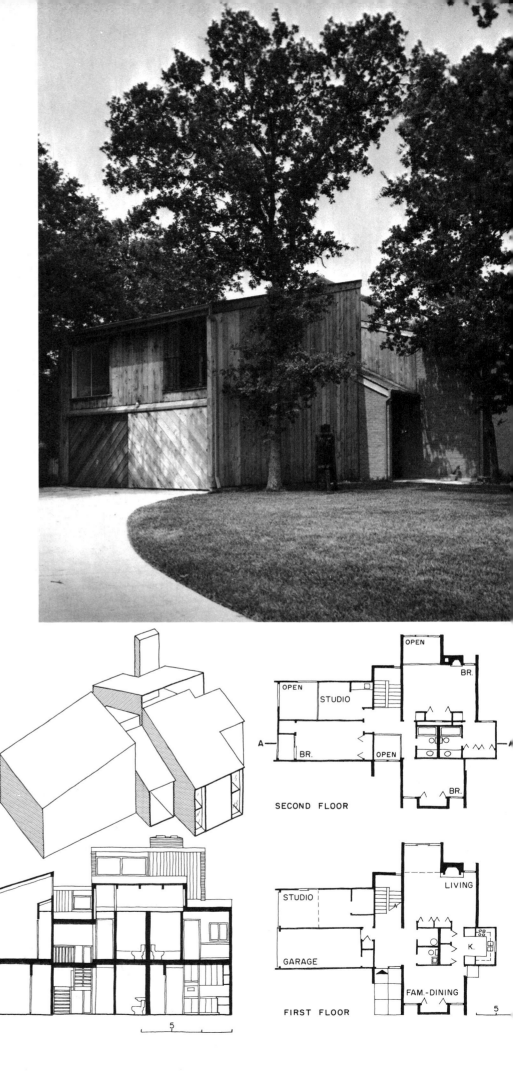

SECOND FLOOR

SECTION A-A

FIRST FLOOR

family-dining room. I started with the core and from there evolved a plan which placed the kitchen and family-dining room on one side, and the living room on the other. Upstairs the master bedroom and one other bedroom are separated by the bathrooms. The hallway had to be minimum, so the entry-stair/hall relationship fell in place. It was at this point that the shed-roof motif seemed appropriate to give me volumetric space, and to allow skylight spaces between the forms."

Mr. Heimsath says that he had some difficulty in deciding how to relate the studio wing with the rest of the house. The massing of the other forms built up into a "counter-thrusting" relationship, but the studio wing had nothing to counter-thrust against. It was therefore turned around "to play off against the rest of the house. Then it worked." The resulting scheme has a rather compact, sculptural effect, but the many skylights give it life and interest and save it from being too inward-looking.

Mr. Heimsath is convinced that no two rooms in one house should have the same spatial impact. By placing storage on the exterior wall of the family room—in contrast to the living room where it is on the interior wall, with the fireplace on the outside—he was able to vary the interior spaces and at the same time provide sufficient exterior massing to offset the dominance of the shed forms.

Architect: Clovis Heimsath; *Owner:* Mr. and Mrs. Robert K. Fowler, Jr.; *Location:* Houston; *Contractor:* W. A. Simmons

A certain amount of flexibility was provided by making the ground-floor studio convertible to a garage if necessary, and the upstairs studio to a fourth bedroom if required. The house is set diagonally on its site, allowing a view up a bayou on one side. From the balcony of the children's bedroom above the garage, there is a pleasant outlook up the tree-lined street. Exterior materials of brick, rough cedar and glass are well detailed and carefully related to each other.

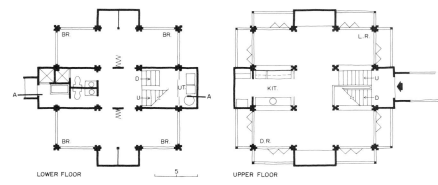

LOWER FLOOR   5   UPPER FLOOR

Julius Shulman photos

When architect Harrell McCarty decided to build himself a house near Hilo, on the island of Hawaii, he had some very clear criteria upon which to base the design. In addition to highly specific environmental circumstances, he planned to construct everything, except for the roof structures and covering, plumbing and wiring, himself.

The complex detailing thus is the loving craftsmanship of the owner and enhances the inherently tropical quality of the roof forms. McCarty points out that climatic conditions near Hilo are rather different from those in Honolulu, where the trade winds are so important. On his site, in addition to almost daily rainfall (nearly eight times the annual precipitation of Honolulu), a consistent daily pattern of on-shore/offshore winds and high humidity dictated a house open to any breeze. Although air conditioning might have solved these problems for a more conventional design, McCarty notes that Hilo has *the* highest electrical power rates in the United States. Furthermore, the sound of the surf nearby was an important reason for building there;

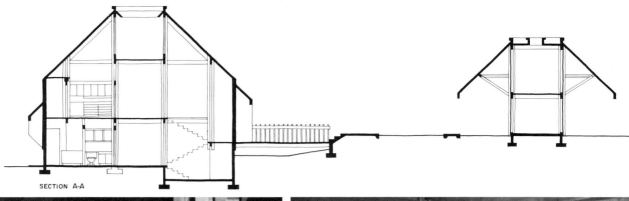

SECTION A-A

windows would have dampened that pleasure considerably.

So the upper floor of the house, already a flexible and open plan as an expression of the McCartys' lifestyle, is surrounded by louvered doors. They can be thrown open in good weather to make the entire space a "lanai," that uniquely Hawaiian concept of protected outdoor living space.

Architect and owner: *Harrell McCarty of Oda/McCarty.* Location: Hilo, Hawaii. Contractor for the structure: *John Lavery.*

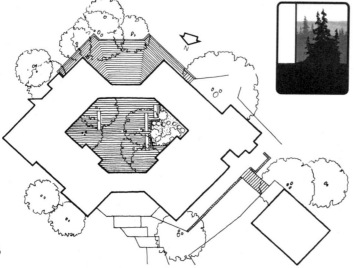

The residence of the Merrill College provost at the University of California, Santa Cruz, is a modest wood building nestled into the redwoods just off the campus. As an official house, it had special program requirements which architects Wong and Brocchini have chosen to fulfill in a relaxed and informal way. Counting on the benign climate of Monterey Bay, they have wrapped the house around a spacious open courtyard in which the provost holds weekly "soup suppers" for groups of the students and staff. The left wing of the plan contains the rooms in which other entertaining and meetings take place while the other L-shaped wing contains the family living space, three children's bedrooms, family room and kitchen.

Architects: WORLEY K. WONG and RONALD G. BROCCHINI of Wong & Brocchini. *Location:* Santa Cruz, California. *Engineers:* Forell/Elsasser Engineers Inc. (structural); Ralston & Dwyer (mechanical/electrical). *Landscape architects:* Royston, Hanamoto, Beck & Abey. *Contractor:* Reese Construction Company.

Joshua Freiwald photos

The site slopes down from the entry (above) and the family room (upper right) so that the deck outside the living and dining rooms (right) is almost seven feet above grade. The distant bay can be seen from there through the trees. The central courtyard is also above grade. In order to minimize damage to the roots of the clump of redwoods within the space (right) the floor is 2 by 6 redwood boards on a light framework. The benches and a buffet table are built-in to serve the outdoor functions. All exterior walls are sheathed with red cedar shingles.

The major rooms of the house all look into the central courtyard, but more importantly, they each have different views out into the magnificent redwood grove in which the house is placed. The entry (left) is a transparent link with passages that lead to family room and library (above). This room can be closed off from the passage and the adjacent living room (right) by sliding doors. The living room and the dining room (below) are the largest and most richly detailed spaces in the house. In addition to the large south-facing glass walls and access to the deck both share, the living room has redwood siding and specially designed cast-stone trim at the fireplace. Bedrooms and other major rooms all have sloping ceilings, which are expressed on the exterior by shed roofs.

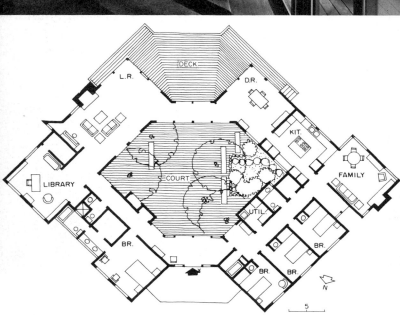

HOUSES IN VACATION PLACES
FOR OCCASIONAL USE

A vacation place is a special place, either because of unique beauty or spectacular location, or because it offers opportunities for recreational activities. The West has all kinds, including skiing in summer. Cabins, vacation houses, and second homes abound in places of beauty or activity. The surroundings can be spectacular or plain; it is the house that translates grandeur of scenery into human terms, and makes the ordinary memorable.

In this section is a selection of houses for some of the varied scenic places in the West—wooded places, open meadows, mountains, and beaches—designed for weekend or occasional use. In addition, because a growing number of people choose to live year round in a vacation place—some because their work is there, others because retirement makes it possible—there is a group of houses designed for permanent residence. What

differentiates these houses from those intended for occasional use is that they provide for special kinds of activities—hobbies—which the occasional house does not need to do; also, the year-round house is usually larger. One of the Sea Ranch houses, for instance, has two full kitchen counters because both husband and wife like to cook, and often do so at the same time (page 174). Another has a greenhouse and a studio (page 178).

Wood, left to weather, is the predominant material used in all these houses, a sensible choice for the climatic conditions to which the houses are exposed, and appropriately simple to handle, both in design and in construction.

IN THE WOODS

About 60 miles north of San Francisco, near the Napa Valley town of St. Helena, this weekend house, of about 1,700 square feet, is set into a hilltop clearing beneath towering pines.

Now and again, one can hear cones and branches fall onto the contour-clutching hip roof, laid up in red cedar shingles, pitching high over good-sized living, entertainment, and sleeping areas.

Because of the slope, the structure steps down, with two levels. At the entranceway, at the end of a mile-long drive, the second level, containing a guest room, protrudes over the front door and, to assure privacy, no other openings are placed on this side of the house. The lower-level living spaces, which the guest room overlooks, are expansive, opening out to the surroundings, and embellished with examples of Bay Area art. In a spatial free-for-all, the living room flows into an affable, kitchen-eating area and, just adjacent, the owner's study.

The planes of resawn, knotty cedar, used outside as well, and the overhead beams of fir, set up a unifying play of surfaces that is anchored in place by a hearth of Feather River travertine (browns, tans) from way up in the Sierras. Sunlight and moonlight take turns with the skylight above the hearth, the room being luminous even after dark when, most usually, beasts can be heard going bump in the night round about the terraces, laid down in local fieldstone and bordered with ferns.

Architect: Kirby Ward Fitzpatrick
   447 Sutter Street
   San Francisco, California
Private residence
Location: St. Helena, California
Landscape architect: Jonathan Herr
Contractor: H.S. Meinberger and Son
Photographer: Jim Ball

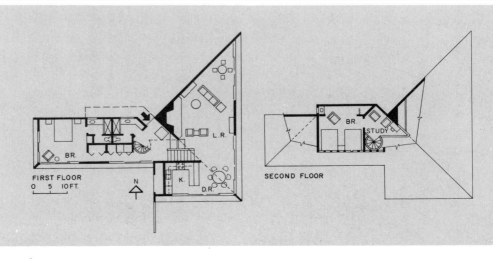

FIRST FLOOR
0 5 10 FT.

SECOND FLOOR

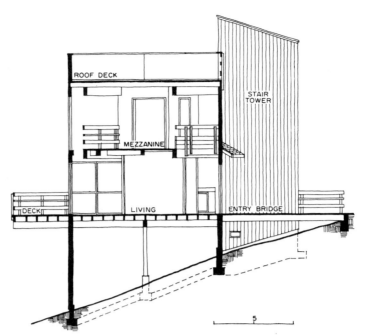

This low-budget vacation house at the Sea Ranch, a complex of vacation homes north of San Francisco, was built as a prototype to show prospective buyers the sort of house that might be built on a steep, heavily wooded hillside lot with a distant view of the water. The house is a festive and simple one-room hexagonal tower with an attached stair tower. The stairs lead to a sleeping-shelf mezzanine with bath, and then on to a roof deck with a magnificent view. The main level, containing living room, kitchen and porch, is entered via a bridge, with the entrance sheltered by a canopy roof. The exterior is horizontally- and vertically-applied redwood treated with bleaching oil; with a built-up roof and duck-board decking. Interior walls are fir and plywood, with ceilings of exposed fir beams and decking of plywood. The house is designed for expansion by adding hexa-gons.

VACATION HOUSE, The Sea Ranch, Sonoma County, California. Owner: *Oceanic Proper-ties.* Architects: *Marquis and Stoller—Peter Kampf, associate.* Engineer: *Eric Elsesser.* Contractor: *Mat-thew Sylvia.*

MEZZANINE FLOOR

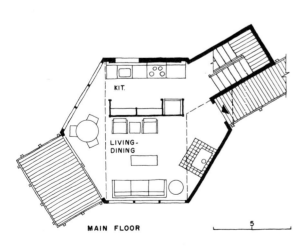

MAIN FLOOR

A sleeping deck overlooks the two-story living room in this vertically-organized octagonal house for a steep, wooded site.

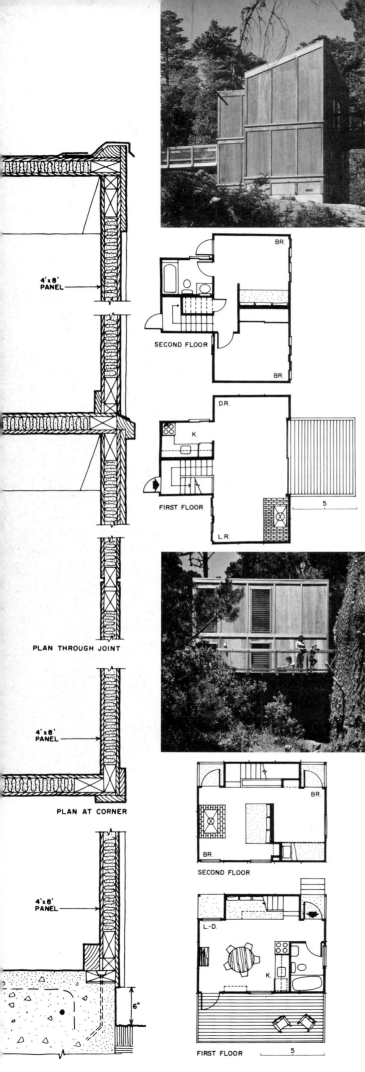

4'x8' PANEL →

PLAN THROUGH JOINT

4'x8' PANEL →

PLAN AT CORNER

4'x8' PANEL →

SECOND FLOOR

BR.

BR.

D.R.

K.

FIRST FLOOR

L.R.

5

SECOND FLOOR

BR.

BR.

L-D.

K.

FIRST FLOOR   5

This rugged and very original little house grew out of an attempt to provide a specially designed low-cost vacation home in a beautiful but remote area where building costs are high. It uses prefabricated stressed-skin panels for walls and floors, for an estimated 15-per cent saving over conventional wood frame. In addition to the house shown at right, two even lower-priced versions have been built, shown at left.

The patented structural panels consist of a plywood skin and a rigid, fire-resistant foam plastic core. The core insulates, and the plywood—redwood on the exterior and cedar or fir inside—also forms the finish.

The panels are four feet wide, and the real key to success came in using this module as the basis for efficient plans. The large house has a 932-square-foot living area. It has a full kitchen and bathroom, wall-to-wall indoor-outdoor carpets and electric floor and baseboard unit heating. The second is a smaller house (top left); and the third, even smaller, was constructed with sleeping alcoves and the use of outdoor decks. Details for all three were designed to scuttle complicated on-site construction steps and use simple joints and simple finishes from stock materials to help keep costs in line. Typical details are shown at far left, from top: a wall section at the roof and through the second floor; a wall-panel joint; a cross-section at a corner; and (bottom) a wall section at the foundation. The battens and fascia double for trim and weathertight joints. Electricity was incorporated in the panels by running a heated rod through the plastic core for wiring chases. The large house took just three days to build, using a four-man crew.

Architects: HIRSHEN & VAN DER RYN
Location: Point Reyes, California
Owner: Sim Van der Ryn
Contractor: W. D. McAlvain

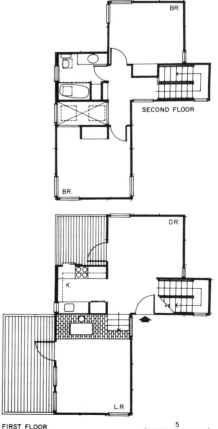

BR.

SECOND FLOOR

BR.

D.R.

K.

L.R.

FIRST FLOOR   5

A number of playful "extras" are built into the two-story, split-level design: The living room with its Franklin stove has a skylit, two-story "well." An overlook from the kitchen can be seen in the photos (below). Wherever possible, outdoor decks are enlisted to increase living space without adding to foundation costs.

Joshua Freiwald photos

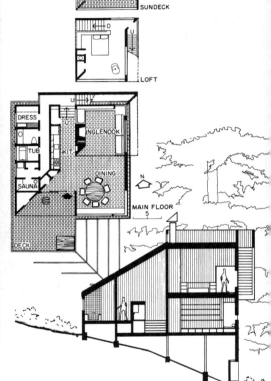

SUNDECK

LOFT

DRESS

INGLENOOK

TUB

KIT

SAUNA

DINING

DECK

N

MAIN FLOOR
5

Jeremiah O. Bragstad photos

An indigenous material and a modest form have been combined to produce an intriguing yet uncomplicated vacation house. Architects McCue Boone Tomsick make the most of a downhill approach (above) by sheathing the roof as well as the walls with tongue-and-groove redwood boards. The unifying effect of the common material makes the house seem smaller and more simple than it proves to be upon entry (opposite). Yet such modesty is entirely appropriate when the site is an isolated and heavily forested hillside in the Santa Cruz Moutains of California, looking out over a valley preserve toward the Pacific Ocean. The angled wall, which follows the hip of the roof at the entry, provides protected entrance where those who have walked down the hill from the parking area may remove muddy boots and winter coats before entering. That part of the house is oriented away from the winds but catches mid-day sun. End-grain redwood paving blocks form a parquet terrace that continues indoors as an important finish.

A very generous stairway within the single, large interior space makes vertical circulation an important generator of the functional relationships. Directly ahead, as one enters, a short flight of steps just past the kitchen leads to the level with four small rooms containing toilet facilities (including a sauna). To the right and up the stairs is the bedroom. Again to the right, and now outdoors, this squared spiral leads up to the sundeck in the treetops. Redwood boards also sheathe the interior completely; the ceiling boards are spaced slightly apart to assist in ventilation of the roof structure. Although the large space is beautifully detailed, it is clear that it was designed for unpretentious and relaxed vacation use. Within the large space, the eating area is adjacent to the strip kitchen. Under the ceiling formed by the bedroom floor, is an inglenook sitting area around a fireplace whose seating doubles as extra sleeping accommodation.

Architects: McCUE BOONE TOMSICK. *Location:* San Mateo County, California. *Engineers:* Hirsh and Gray (structural); Marion, Cerbatos and Tomasi (mechanical/electrical). *General contractor:* Henry Knutzen Sons, Inc.

A high degree of spatial integration is achieved within the house by the use of a single material—redwood—on walls, ceilings and floors. The square spiral stairway and the loft bedroom which opens onto the large space below also contribute to the unified feeling. Butted glazing in both downhill corner windows of the main-floor room provide splendid diagonal views into the thick foliage while the slit windows illuminate the page for anyone reading on the built-in couch.

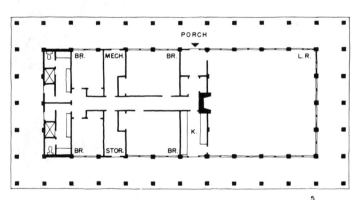

Rugged materials form a weekend hunting lodge for a large Texas working ranch. Set among oak trees on the edge of a man-made, sand-bottom lake, the house aptly echoes its antecedents in low, horizontal lines, straightforward comfort and a usable surrounding porch. A big living-dining area, flanked by a small galley-type kitchen, is at one end of the plan; two combination dressing rooms and baths are at the other end and four bedrooms are in the center. Every room opens to the porch.

The architect uses glass walls, protected by the porch, to open every room to the lake and the ranch acreage beyond; extension of the ceiling and floor materials into the porch area helps further to visually link indoors and outdoors. The living room has an exposed-beam ceiling and brick fireplace. Most surfaces have natural finishes: cedar board and batten exteriors, charcoal-stained cedar posts, teak paneling in the living room and painted pine boards for all other interiors.

RANCH HOUSE, Wallis, Texas. Engineers: *Cunningham and Lemus;* contractor: *Koenig Construction Co.*

SECTION III
HOUSES
IN VACATION
PLACES FOR
OCCASIONAL
USE

OPEN
SITES

The "Binker Barn," named for the salesman who came up with the idea, is repeatable in several different versions. The basic shape is a heavy-framed box, with a kitchen and living areas on the first floor (opposite), two bedrooms and a bath above, and, higher still, lofts for sleeping, or simply for retreat. The lean-to (below) can be a carport, a garage, or a third bedroom with bath. Or a separate garage can be added, as in the more distant of the two versions on the left.

A. Youngmeister photos

This ingenious vacation house has been built well over a dozen times at the Sea Ranch in California. The basic notion is simplicity itself: a barn-like space with a plan that can be flipped and with an appended lean-to whose function is variable. The working out of the notion, though, assures that simplicity does not lead to dullness.

The ground-floor plan is circuitous, so that the apparent size of the space is increased because the eye can never see all of it at once. The "Z"-shaped plan of the second floor allows sunlight to fall into the living areas from skylights in the roof, casting patterns that change with the hours and the seasons. It also provides upward vistas from below, and the pleasure of moving from a low space, like the dining area, to one that is dramatically higher. One can also move outside the enclosing walls of the house to lounge in a bay window, or right up to the peak of the roof to doze or sleep in one of the lofts there. What begins, then, as a simple space ends up providing an admirable array of different places to be and things to do.

The architects assumed that in a vacation house choices of what do and where to do it would be made casually, and so the feeling of the interior is relaxed. The details are simple, the rough-sawn boards are left unfinished, and the heavy framing members stand fully exposed.

Outside, this way of building produces an effect that is downright modest, recalling simple rural structures. It has turned out that, at the Sea Ranch, this assumption of modesty was wise, for as more and more houses are built on the open meadows, each more obviously "designed" than the next, and each one competing with all the others for attention, there is the danger that the place may begin to look more like a statuary farm than the beautifully desolate landscape which it once was, and which the original developers, planners and architects had sought with great care to preserve.

Architects: WILLIAM TURNBULL AND CHARLES MOORE of MLTW / Moore-Turnbull—Robert Theel, associate. *Location:* The Sea Ranch, California. *Engineers:* Patrick Morreau (structural); Brelje and Race (civil). *Contractor:* Matthew D. Sylvia.

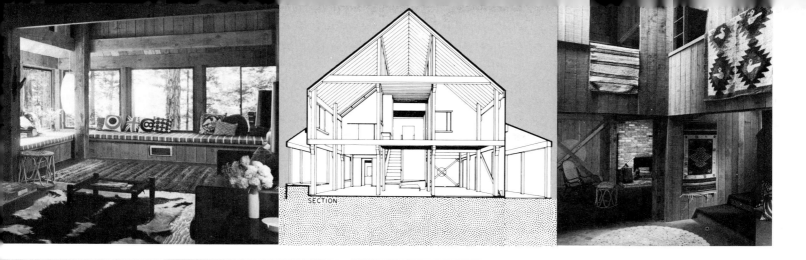

SECTION

LOFT

SECOND FLOOR

FIRST FLOOR

OPEN

LOFT

LOFT

BR

OPEN

D

OPEN

BR

BR

KIT

D R

L R

U

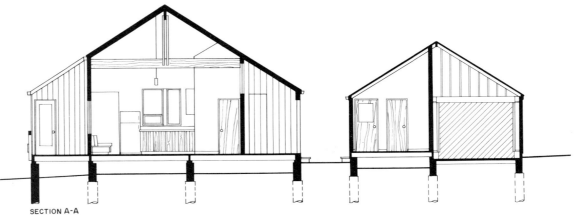

SECTION A-A

A house on the meadow at the Sea Ranch is a highly visible object, exposed to view from the hills and from the highway that separates meadow and hills. In such an open landscape, the size, form and color of a building are unusually important since they determine the degree of contrast between building and land.

The two buildings that make up this unpretentious weekend house are simple in form and color, and, in their straightforward use of rough-sawn stained wood, have the pleasant indigenous look of an old weathered barn. The smaller of the two buildings, now used as a studio-study and a garage, served as living quarters while the main building was under construction. The two principal requirements of the clients were simplicity and privacy for themselves and their three teen-age children. Locating the bedrooms at either end of the big room was a logical—though to the clients, unconventional—way of obtaining privacy, but the clients readily accepted it and found that it worked out well not only for the family but when the house is rented, as it often is, since two couples can occupy it and still have privacy. Guests are provided for in the main building; for an overflow number, window seats convert to bunks, and an aerie above one of the bedrooms can be used for sleeping. The big room, with a view to the ocean at one end and an open kitchen at the other, is the gathering place for everyone. With commendable understanding of the character of the place, the owners have allowed the indigenous wild grasses to grow up to the buildings.

RESIDENCE FOR GLEN NIMNICHT, The Sea Ranch, California. Architect: *Fred L. Osmon.* Engineer: *Harold Davis* (structural). Contractor: *Rick Gladjo.*

Merg Ross photos

144

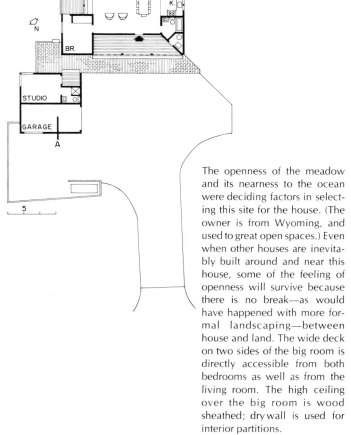

The openness of the meadow and its nearness to the ocean were deciding factors in selecting this site for the house. (The owner is from Wyoming, and used to great open spaces.) Even when other houses are inevitably built around and near this house, some of the feeling of openness will survive because there is no break—as would have happened with more formal landscaping—between house and land. The wide deck on two sides of the big room is directly accessible from both bedrooms as well as from the living room. The high ceiling over the big room is wood sheathed; drywall is used for interior partitions.

Unlike some houses at The Sea Ranch, the renowned private housing development 100 miles north of San Francisco, this house is quite small—approximately 900 square feet—but thanks to its design, it provides amply for the owners who use it for weekends and vacations. The house is located on the crest of the range of wooded hills behind the coastal meadows of The Sea Ranch.

The house is well sited for the conditions of its site: the wedge-shaped lot had an existing driveway entrance on the west, and a stand of well-developed trees on the north. By setting the house against the trees, it was possible to gain a glimpse through the trees of the Pacific Ocean—the only view of it from the site. The orientation on an east-west axis, with the house facing onto an open meadow to the south, brings daylight into the house through the entrance, several windows, and a skylight. The nicely scaled barn-like form with its high shed roofs makes an appropriate

transition from meadow to tall trees, and provides a high-ceilinged interior that belies the small area of the house.

Standard wall construction was used for economy, but in order to strengthen the structure for earthquake resistance, diagonal bracing was also used and incorporated into the design, with particularly dramatic effect at the corner of the dining area where the braces make an interesting juncture. As clearly visible on the outside as in the interior, the bracing is an unexpected and stimulating element in the design of the house.

The L-shaped deck on the south side provides much-used outdoor space, protected from the prevailing strong coastal winds. Redwood boards, set vertically, are used for exterior siding, with redwood shingles used on the roof.

THE GOECKER RESIDENCE, The Sea Ranch, California. Architect: *Donald Jacobs*. Structural engineer: *Fook Z. Lee*. General contractor: *Jay Baker*.

An excitement is generated in the interior spaces by the architect's positioning of a skylight and windows and the exposed structural cross-bracing, focused in the dining room (below). Views from the front of the house are shielded from the parking area by a six-foot-high fence. A skylight and two clerestory windows on the south side are placed so that "light moves around the space," the architect says, spotlighting the dining area in the morning. The sleeping loft is left open to the lower level, but a study on the main floor can be closed off by sliding wood barn doors. Small design subtleties—a window bay with seat on the west side which expands the living area both visually and actually; exposed columns which define spaces and modulate the open interior—play an important role in giving the small interior its air of spaciousness. Yet the interior also has a sense of intimacy, derived from the enclosing trees. Douglas fir boards are used as facing for walls on the interior. Columns are also of Douglas fir.

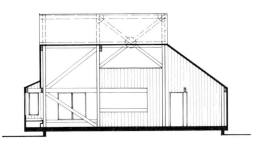

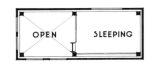

UPPER LEVEL

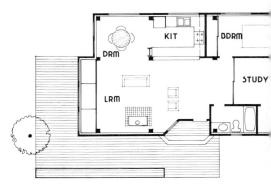

FLOOR PLAN

0   5   10

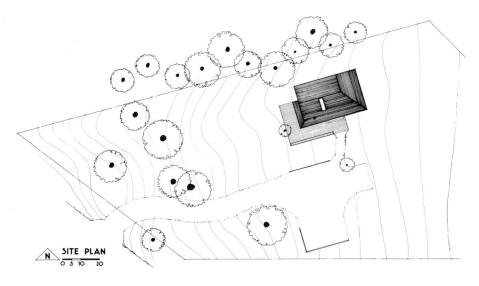

N   SITE PLAN
0 5 10   20

This modest house, carefully sited in a relatively empty stretch of desert north of Phoenix, was designed by its owner and constructed with the help of friends in just over a month, using the simplest kinds of materials and details. A good deal of forethought and invention went into its planning, however. The result is an unusually expressive small house and studio that are fine-tuned to the climate and which were constructed on a very modest budget.

The house is conventionally framed in wood stud with 2 x 10 floor joists supporting a fiberboard subfloor. The roof structure is composed of 3 x 8 fir beams on 4-foot centers. Insulation is applied throughout: 4-inch batts in the stud walls and a 2-inch thickness of rigid urethane under the red roll roofing. The exterior, though, is unexpectedly clad in galvanized metal sheet. Because it is corrugated and matte finished, it does not throw off eye-searing reflections under the bright sun. Instead, it produces softly glowing reflections of the surrounding desert—reflections that change perceptibly as the days and seasons pass.

To the right in the plan (above) is a small drafting studio with two work spaces. Opposite the studio, across the entry breezeway, is the main living space, which also doubles for dining and sleeping. It backs against a kitchen, bath and dressing area. Nearly every space is detailed for multiple use.

Unifying the two halves of the structure is a generously scaled, trellised deck that faces a deep arroyo and undisturbed natural desert beyond. Here is the outdoor center of activity, a space for a wide variety of uses day or night. This north exposure is completely glazed while the openings on the other three elevations are sharply controlled against the sun.

Space conditioning is achieved by an evaporative cooling unit with exposed ducts and a fireplace augmented by portable heaters for winter evenings.

Architect and owners:
  Mr. & Mrs. William P. Bruder
  Black Canyon Stage
  New River, Arizona
Photographer: Neil Koppes

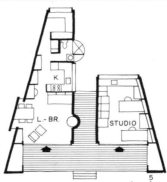

The shallow pitch of the roof is echoed in the tapered plan shapes which open to the north. The large glazed opening is shielded from the sun by an overhead trellis that casts elaborate shadow patterns across the deck and side walls.

This unusual house was built for a college professor and his wife as a weekend retreat for study and the quiet enjoyment of natural surroundings in California's Napa Hills. The architects' solution largely blanks the front to provide the seclusion wanted, and opens the back with glass and a full-length deck to exploit the potential of the site and view. The structure, simply shaped as it is, can be totally closed by a sliding door in front, and by panels, sliding up from under the deck in back, making the house worry-free when the owners are away. The use of shed roofs and cantilevering, and exposed beams and plank ceilings, contributed to its reasonable cost.

Residence for Dr. and Mrs. Herwin Schaefer, Napa Hills, California. Architects: *Marquis and Stoller—Pete Kampf, associate;* contractor: *Vienop Builders.*

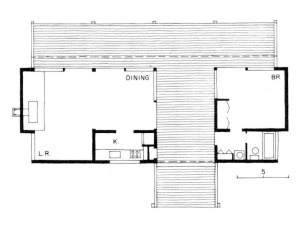

SECTION III
HOUSES
IN VACATION
PLACES FOR
OCCASIONAL
USE

IN THE MOUNTAINS

The majestic site and the minimal support conditions it afforded were prime determinants in the design of this Colorado mountain cabin. Four 16-inch-diameter caissons, each anchored eight feet into bedrock, support a central wedge form that houses the main living area. Steel braces from these caissons pick up the roof loads and floor cantilevers of the two satellite wedge forms. This family of interlocking elements creates a lively and intricate geometry—a theme playfully developed by triangular window openings—but the use of a single exterior finish material—1- by 6-inch redwood siding on walls and roofs—gives the massing a welcome homogeneity. Adding to this unity is a constant roof slope of 3 on 2, which ends up in a volume of strongly vertical spatial development.

The cabin is structured of 2- by 6-inch studs sheathed on both sides with ½-inch plywood glued and nailed to form a stressed-skin panel. The plywood, taped and painted white, is the primary interior finish material.

The exterior walls are sandwiched with 6-inch batts of glass fiber, which give sufficient insulation to heat the entire cabin with electric baseboard heaters of 58,-000 Btu/hr capacity.

The owners asked that the cabin disturb the natural beauty of the site as little as possible. They got their wish—and a great deal more.

Architects: Arley Rinehart Associates
  2345 Seventh Street
  Denver, Colorado
Clients: Mr. and Mrs. Ben Collins
Present owners: Dr. and Mrs.
  Nelson E. Mohler
Location: Perry Park, Colorado
Engineers:
  Ron Frickel (structural)
  J. J. Blank (mechanical)
  R. W. Thompson (foundation)
Contractor: Ben Collins
Photographers: Richard Springgate,
  Robert McConnell

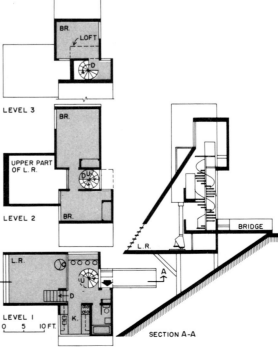

LEVEL 3

LEVEL 2

LEVEL 1
0 5 10 FT.

SECTION A-A

This rustic yet sophisticated mountain cabin near Mt. Rainier skillfully uses Douglas fir and stone available from the 40-acre tract. Architect Alan Liddle designed, constructed, and built the cabin over a period of years for his own use. The materials blend well with the environment, making it an ideal weekend and vacation retreat.

Designed for a ledge halfway up a cliff, the cabin's scheme evolved from the terrain itself, with the living room the first stage, and two wings with kitchen and bedroom added later. Finished cedar and hemlock paneling were used in the interiors. The entire cost was low, with all construction done by the architect himself, including most built-in furnishings.

Mountain Cabin, Mt. Rainier, Washington. Architect and owner: *Alan Liddle*.

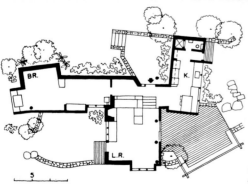

Charles R. Pearson photos

156

Designed expressly for the snow conditions of ski country, this family lodge derives its strong shape from an outward slope of the upper walls, which is planned to prevent ice dams and allow run-off from melting snows to fall clear of the house. View decks are provided at various levels and double as entrances in exceptionally deep snows.

The plan is a multi-level scheme, with a variety of inter-related spaces: some are low-ceilinged, snug areas; others are two stories in height and overlooked by balcony rooms. All the interiors are comfortable, bright and easy to maintain. Much of the furniture is built in.

Residence for Dr. and Mrs. Sanford H. Lazar, Squaw Valley, California. Architect: *Gerald Gamliel Weisbach*; contractor: *Earl Kelley.*

FIRST FLOOR

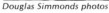

Douglas Simmonds photos

SECOND FLOOR   5

158

SECTION III
HOUSES
IN VACATION
PLACES FOR
OCCASIONAL
USE

ON THE BEACH

This house on the sparsely settled north coast of California is both a weekend and vacation house for its owners and a retreat for longer periods from their small flat on Telegraph Hill in San Francisco, an hour's drive away. The site is a 60-by 450-foot plot, at the base of the coast range, with an unobstructed view of the ocean from the front and of the 2000-foot ridge, half a mile inland, from the back. All the principal spaces have one or the other of these views.

Since the owners spend much of their time at the beach outdoors, the house is also planned for a free and casual relationship between interior and exterior spaces. In contrast to the open terraces on both ocean and ridge sides of the house, the patio is a carefully controlled exterior environment, enclosed by two pairs of high gates, front and back, between the house and the studio block, which give privacy and protection from the strong winds of this section of the coast. Within the 24- by 24-foot patio, plants provide seasonal color and variety of texture: outside the patio, beach grass is allowed to grow up to the house. A vegetable garden is located behind the house. The house is in two parts—living spaces in the main building, two studio workshops in a separate structure. The living-dining-kitchen area is designed to a scale that is comfortable for two people or, on occasion, for a larger number of people. Essentially, these two parts are boxes whose volumes are controlled by the dimensions of the resawn-redwood plywood panels (10 foot, standard, with grooves 4 inches apart) used throughout. Details are consistent: standard sliding residential door units connect major rooms and patio; exterior trim is all-heart solid redwood; the roof structure is a system of beams and decking, and the same trim is used at the termination of the sheetrock wall finish just below the roof framing; interiors are painted all white.

Architect: Morton Rader
    of Chan/Rader & Associates
    710 Sansome Street
    San Francisco, California
Private residence
Location: Marin County, California
Engineers:
    Stefan Medwadowski (structural)
    Charles & Braun and
    Montgomery & Roberts (mechanical)
    Mazzetti & Parish (electrical)
Interior and landscape design:
    Morton Rader and Betty Bird
Contractors: Edward W. Burger, Inc.
Photographer: Bernard Poinssot

The patio is the heart of the house and its carefully controlled environment
is regulated by the high gates, at front and rear, which provide for privacy
or open to the views to ocean and ridge, and protect from wind.

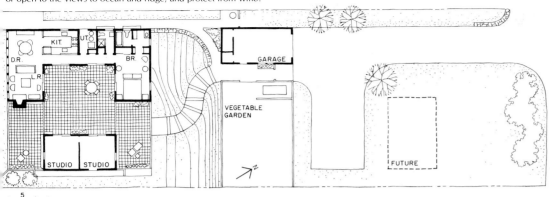

Dense with vegetation, the site is a narrow strip that separates a freshwater pond from a gravel beach facing Puget Sound to the north. The architect's intention was to site this year-round vacation house as far back from the beach as possible, opening views north and south through the thick natural cover.

The plan is appealing in its simplicity. Half the house is set off for living, dining, relaxing—in one space that incorporates both views. A food preparation area is set along one wall and can be screened off with two sliding barn doors. The other half of the house includes the two bedrooms separated by two baths. Space for a small laundry, accessible from outside, is borrowed from both bathrooms. This whole section of the house, as well as the north portion of the living room (left in plan), is sheltered by a pitched roof. High clerestories under the roof pitch bring diffused daylight into the bedrooms and baths and provide closely framed views into surrounding treetops.

All glass is fixed with ventilation panels above the windows in the living area and above the soffit line in the bedrooms. Oak strip floors have been lightly sanded and oiled. Inside and out, the principal finish is rough-sawn cedar applied vertically over a standard wood frame. Barn doors, mounted on long rails, provide an easy means of closing the house when not in use or protecting its occupants from the severe storms that occasionally make their way down the Strait.

The same modesty and restraint that characterizes the house design was applied in choosing plant materials. Everything is indigenous. Sword ferns, vine maple and aspen, among others, were transplanted from the nearby woods to mend the minimal scars left by construction.

Architect: Richard Cardwell
    Pier 64
    Seattle, Washington
Owners: Mr. & Mrs. H. H. Griggs
Contractor: Nelson Lumber
Photographer: Larry Hutson

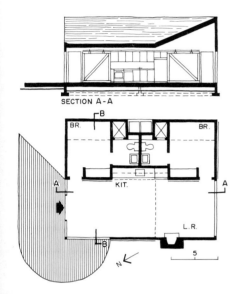

SECTION A-A

The roof pitch turns 90 degrees over the owner's bedroom creating an interesting geometry not easy to read in every elevation. Photo at far right is taken across the freshwater pond toward the Straits.

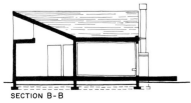

SECTION B-B

Christian Staub photos

The site: Crane Island in Puget Sound's San Juan Islands. The architect and owner: Wendell Lovett. His program: a small, low-maintenance vacation retreat for his own family that would provide a holiday atmosphere and a complete change from urban routine.

The resulting structure is only 12 feet wide and contains just 370 square feet of enclosed space including a small sleeping loft reached from inside by a simple ladder-stair. Inverted bow-string trusses support the roof and suspend the deck that cantilevers 18 feet over the foundations. Within this structure, Lovett has fitted a compact kitchen, plumbing essentials, minimum storage and space for sitting and sleeping

six. All furniture is built in. The level of the deck drops one step (the depth of the joists—see section) inside to accommodate the mattress seating.

Much of the fun of this house comes from the boldness of the concept: the tightness of the plan contrasted against the audacity of the long cantilever, as well as from the skill with which the house exploits the site and view. The detailing is neat and clean throughout but never fussy, and retains a very pleasant and appropriate sense of informality.

In form and color, the interiors carry through the design theme stated so simply and forcefully on the exteriors. There is no wasted motion in the design and hardly a

space or element that is not put to multiple use. The house is conceived and executed in rare singleness of purpose, and realizes admirably the design goals of its program, taking advantage of the beautiful site without harming it, and achieving its intentions with an economy of means as well as of cost.

All structural lumber is Douglas fir. Exterior and interior cladding is rough-sawn cedar stained to match the bark of surrounding trees.

LOVETT VACATION HOUSE, Crane Island, Washington. Architect: *Wendell Lovett*. Structural engineer: *Robert Albrecht*. Contractor, *architect with Clifford I. Hooper.*

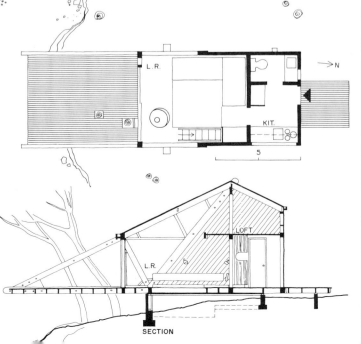

L.R.

KIT.

N

5

LOFT

L.R.

SECTION

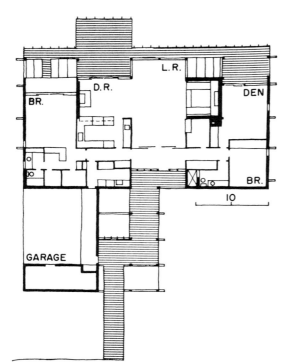

A year-round beach house beautifully situated at the southern end of Puget Sound takes full advantage of an impressive site while avoiding any conflict with the scenery. A broad, sheltered deck extends the house to the water's edge. The main rooms face the water and open to it. Even the entrance, at one end of the living room but separated from it by sliding glass doors, has a view through to the Sound. The simple rectangular plan with its well-ordered spaces and imaginative details—the clerestory windows, the hearthside seating alcove by the stone fireplace, the set-back waterside bedroom—is handled with restraint and grace.

Residence for Mr. and Mrs. William L. Dafoe, Longbranch, Washington. Architects: Kirk, Wallace, McKinley Associates; Structural consultants: Worthington, Skilling, Helle & Jackson; Mechanical consultants: James B. Notkin & Associates; Contractor: Leo Heather; Landscape architect: Richard Yamasaki.

Hugh N. Stratford photos

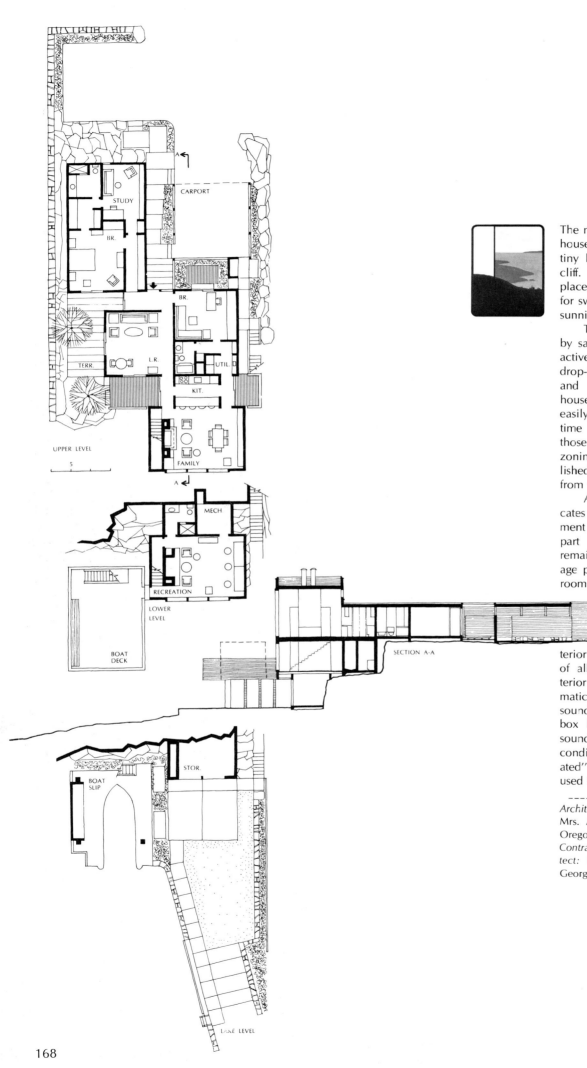

STUDY

CARPORT

BR.

BR.

TERR.

L.R.

UTIL.

KIT.

FAMILY

UPPER LEVEL

5

A

MECH

RECREATION

LOWER LEVEL

BOAT DECK

SECTION A-A

STOR.

BOAT SLIP

LAKE LEVEL

The many functions of an active lakeshore house are amply provided for here on a tiny lot which is split by a 25-foot rock cliff. This is a house of many different places—for eating, for visiting, for privacy, for swimming, for boating, for dancing, for sunning.

The architect describes the program by saying "this lake community is a very active social area, with much informal, drop-in-type entertaining by both adults and teenagers. The owners wanted a house that would function naturally and easily in this situation, while at the same time affording a measure of privacy to those family members wishing it. Thus zoning and sound control was established as a major factor—against noises from within or without the house."

A glance at the plan quickly indicates how a somewhat unusual arrangement of the various rooms plays a large part in assuring that the parents' study remains quiet and peaceful during teenage parties in the family room, recreation room or boat deck.

Noise transmission is also combatted by lining the house with sound-insulation board, which is used on both sides of all interior partitions, ceilings, and the inside of all exterior walls. In addition, all interior doors are equipped with "automatic door bottoms" to seal against sound; convenience outlets and switch box locations were chosen to minimize sound carry-through; heating and air-conditioning ducts are "sound attenuated"; and a double-studded partition is used to isolate bedroom and bath.

Architect: Edgar Wilson Smith. *Owners:* Mr. and Mrs. Art J. Priestley. *Location:* Lake Oswego, Oregon. *Structural engineer:* Bernard L. Tiland. *Contractor:* Bernard & Kinney. *Landscape architect:* Robert Hale Ellis, Jr. *Interior designer:* George M. Schwarz, Jr. and Associates.

Edmund Y. Lee photos

On the central Oregon coast at Salishan a beach-house complex, designed by and for the architectural office of Travers/Johnston as a retreat, has been successfully created as "another world . . . a world I wish we could share with all," says Stephen Johnston. As a tribute to the delightful character of the retreat, it has been in almost constant use by the architects and employees and their families, clients and friends.

Located on the end lot of a spit of land separating Siletz Bay from the Pacific Ocean, the site has a commanding and uninterrupted 270-degree view of water. After the idea of a retreat was decided upon, the office staff was asked for suggestions, with the final design concept arrived at after many idea exchanges. The two major requirements were that it must be a retreat which would allow places for solitude as well as group gatherings, and that it accommodate several families at the same time. This need for a variety of spaces spurred the idea of an octagonal lodge and three hexagonal bedroom units (or modules), grouped in

An exhilarating site for a retreat, the Salishan Spit is sand dunes stabilized by pines, grasses and logs swept onto the beaches. Comprising 2000 sq ft, the retreat does not intrude on the area. The only landscaping needed was to reestablish native grasses and pines surrounding the complex.

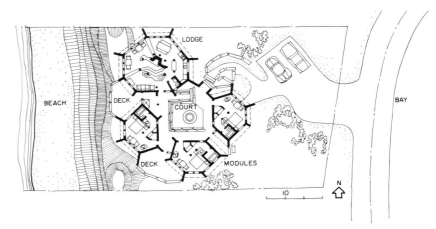

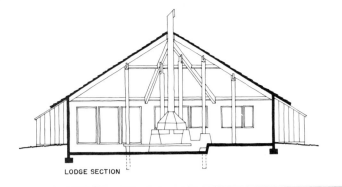

LODGE SECTION

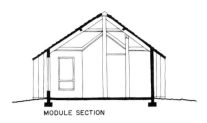

MODULE SECTION

The lodge (left), as the center for most group activities, has the only kitchen, dining and lounge areas. Changes in floor level, expressed in carpet-covered concrete steps, form seating around the fire-pit and contribute to the informality of the room. The bedroom modules are identical. Two modules have views of dunes and one has an ocean view.

a circle to create a central courtyard onto which all doors open. The focal point of the courtyard is a sunken area where guests can sit around an open fire-pit. Two decks on the ocean side provide space for sunning. A basement under one module serves as boat shed, laundry and storage area.

At the angles of each unit are fins extending outward. This element of the design is a strong exterior feature, visually unifying the buildings and serving as a partial windscreen against the strong and almost constant winds.

The exterior is of resawn cedar with a roof of cedar shingles. To capture the magnificent views of land and water and to allow as much light as possible to enter on the foggy and stormy days that are so much a part of the Northwest coast's weather, glass doors and many large windows are used. Glass partitions between units also serve as additional windscreens and open up views to the courtyard. The largest of the modules, the lodge, provides such necessary community facilities as kitchen, eating and lounging areas. Smooth cedar

is used on interior walls, resawn hemlock on the ceiling. The communal character of the project is emphasized by the fact that the whole complex was not only designed but built by the architects and their staff.

BEACH HOUSE-RETREAT, Salishan, Glenedon Beach, Oregon. Architects: *Travers/Johnston.* Engineers: *MacKenzie Engineering Inc.* (structural), *Hugh L. Langton & Associates* (electrical), *McGinnis Engineering Inc.* (mechanical). Interiors: *Travers/Johnston.* Landscape architect: *William Teufel.* Contractor: *Trajon Corporation.*

SECTION III
HOUSES
IN VACATION
PLACES FOR

YEAR-ROUND USE

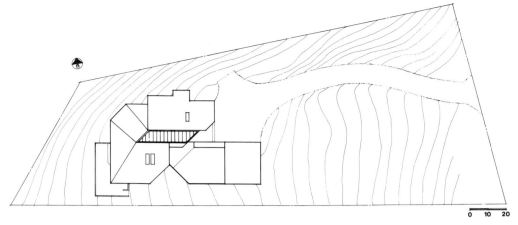

 The site is a highly visible, open hillside with magnificent views of the Pacific Ocean and the rugged northern California coast. The house is set on the lower portion of the property to obtain as sweeping a panorama as possible, since trees and large bushes to the north would have obscured part of the view had the house been situated on the upper portion. A row of pines to south and west filters the view in that direction and screens the house. In response to the nature of the place and to minimize intrusion of the house on the site, the profile of the structure is kept low, and the pitch of the roofs visually ties the house to the land. To continue the character set by the first buildings at The Sea Ranch, the house has an almost stark look, to which details—no overhangs, no moldings on any of the openings—as well as the plain board siding contribute. Although deck space is provided on the sunny sides, west and south, the most usable outdoor space is a partially protected courtyard on the east between the studio and garage. The angled courtyard fence, at the southeast corner of the studio, breaks the line of the house on the south side. There was little disturbance of indigenous grasses and plants and the owners have retained the natural landscaping. The use of redwood siding and cedar shingles, left to weather, help to relate the house to its natural surroundings.

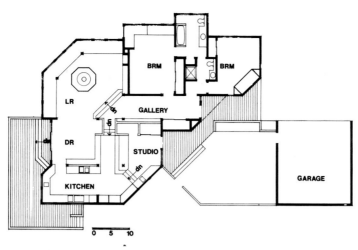

The open plan, variations in ceiling heights, and a change in levels create a feeling of spaciousness in the main living areas. The entrance gallery, bedrooms and a studio for Mrs. Barrell are located on the upper level; and the living room, dining room and kitchen are on a level a few feet lower. The owners wanted "no dark places" in the interiors, so skylights were placed where light was needed most. The largest skylight, running the length of the entrance gallery, allows abundant light to fill the entry hall and provide the "warm welcome" the owners asked for, to flow into the interior of the living room, and to light the walkway between the studio and dining room. The length of the hall affords display space for the owners' rugs and for books. The main living areas are oriented to views on the north, west and south through a band of windows which bring the view "into scale with the individual," a particular request of the owners. Rough-sawn red cedar walls and fir ceilings give warmth to the interiors and help relate them to the outside surroundings. Bronze-tinted glass in the main living areas cuts glare.

RESIDENCE FOR MR. & MRS. RICHARD BARRELL, The Sea Ranch, California. Architect: *Donald Jacobs.* Structural engineer: *Fook Z. Lee.* General contractor: *Mathew D. Sylvia.*

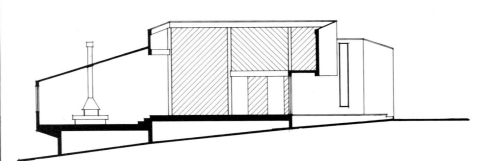

A greenhouse for winter gardening was a natural connector between the house and the studio, where the owners work and hold small classes. Then, greenhouse sections suggested themselves as an equally natural way to provide openness and light throughout. They are stacked and staggered to admit light into both floors of the house (left), or used singly to light the entrance hall or to cover a projecting balcony.

Resawn cedar plywood and pre-fabricated greenhouse sections are the key visual elements in this combination house and studio nestled into the Santa Cruz Mountains of California. The owners are two artists and teachers who preferred to live casually in a house that gave them a sense of openness and light. They also wanted to garden, maintain a small orchard, and keep horses; and they didn't want to have to worry about using their house as a base for these kinds of activities.

The stock greenhouse sections seem pleasantly domestic, even though it is possible to see in them recollections of the finely honed work of James Stirling. The interior spaces, too, must owe something to cousins at The Sea Ranch, and the rough plywood finish is an easy-going industrial counterpart to the kinds of materials Ray Region architects have favored for years. Yet the house manages to be powerfuly different. It is indi-vidualistic, even good-naturedly homely, and it is brimming over with the sense that it is just the kind of house its owners wanted, and knew they could not get pre-packaged.

It was they, in fact, who or-dered the plywood finish. It was also they who found themselves, as the designs were being worked out, in the familiar *cul-de-sac* of wanting more than they could af-ford, and not being willing to build in stages. So they rolled up their sleeves and built the house them-selves, with assistance from the architect and only one full-time carpenter.

The house is a cheering ex-pression of the owners' special taste, and of their architect's abil-ity to nourish it. The architect let the house not only be different, but also quietly and blessedly unrhe-torical; this is a quality to be greatly treasured.

Architect: PETER BEHN of Behn and Gavin. *Owners:* Mr. and Mrs. Robert Lozano. *Location:* Santa Cruz County, California.

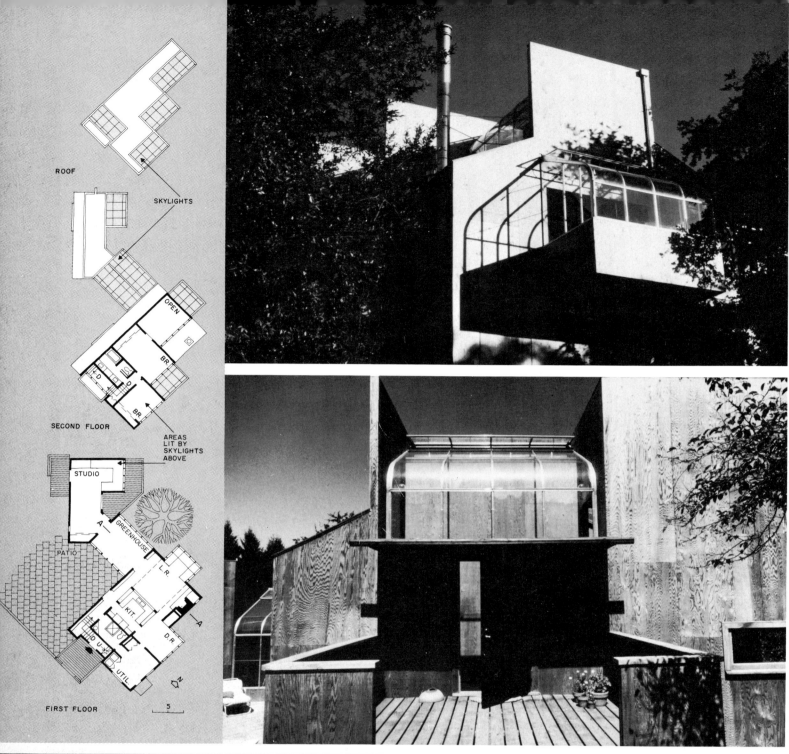

ROOF

SKYLIGHTS

SECOND FLOOR

AREAS
LIT BY
SKYLIGHTS
ABOVE

STUDIO

GREENHOUSE

PATIO

L.R.

KIT.

D.R.

UTIL

FIRST FLOOR

5

Inside the house, cedar plywood remains the finish material, and there is an abundance of natural light in all of the rooms. A bedroom and a bath on the second floor are shown on the right above; adjacent on the right is the greenhouse, seen through sliding barn doors. Above and on the left is the living room, lit by two greenhouse sections, and penetrated from the second floor of the house by a small balcony.

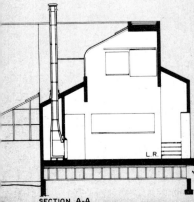

SECTION A-A

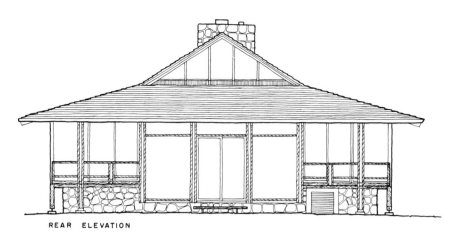

REAR ELEVATION

Wood, stone and the outdoors were the most powerful factors in determining the design of this house, which started with the tremendous advantage of a magnificent site on the front range of the Rockies near Boulder. Since the clients had deliberately moved out of the city to find seclusion in the mountains, they were naturally anxious to retain all the original features of the land, particularly the pine trees. Openings in several parts of the roof overhang allow the trees near the house to grow undisturbed, and are a very direct expression of the close relationship between house and site.

Architect Hobart Wagener rejected any temptation to compete with the surroundings and concentrated—most successfully—on designing a simple, logical structure "which would try to become an integral part of the site." For this purpose, cedar beveled siding and cedar shake roof were a good choice because of their attractive weathering quality. A bleaching oil finish was used on the walls to accelerate the natural process.

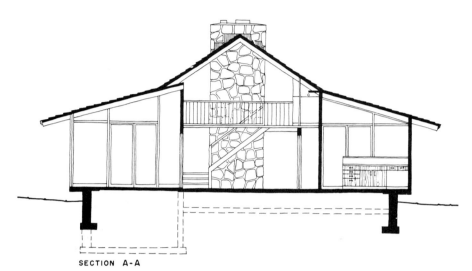

SECTION A-A

The sense of shelter and security needed in a fairly rugged setting is provided by placing the main seating area in a "well" between a raised terrace on one side and a raised dining area on the other, by the use of warm-colored brick for the floors, segmentation of the large glass areas, and the protective roof overhang all around the house.

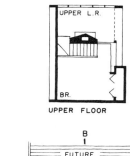

UPPER FLOOR

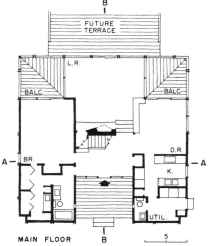

MAIN FLOOR

The interior is dominated by an enormous stone fireplace, an exposed ceiling structure and a dramatic view of the valley. Strategically placed clerestory windows highlight the effect of the ceiling formation and also point up the detailing of the fireplace stonework.

The house is small—with only one full bedroom on the first floor and a guest balcony behind the fireplace—but outdoor decks, the added height in the center of the house, and of course the view, extend the experience of space beyond its walls.

In addition to space and freedom, an exposed site of this kind demands warmth, shelter and a sense of permanence. This was fully recognized by the architect in the careful balance of openness and enclosure and in his sensitive exploitation of the strong, textural quality of natural materials.

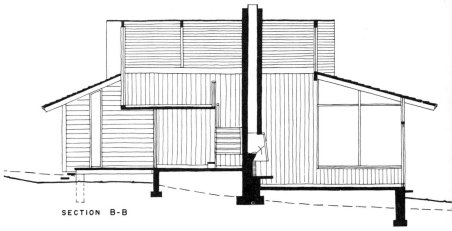

SECTION B-B

Architects: Hobart D. Wagener Associates—*associate on job:* Robert E. Carlson. *Owners:* Mr. and Mrs. A. J. Bartkus. *Location:* Boulder, Colorado. *Contractor:* Warren R. Slattendale.

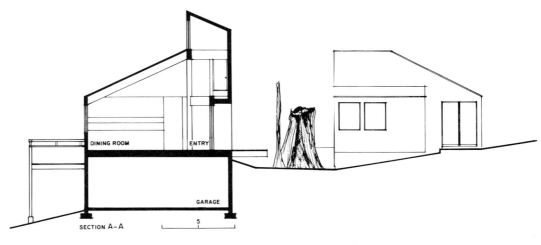

SECTION A-A 5

On the hills at The Sea Ranch, most house sites are out of view among trees and bushes, although some—on the slope of the hill facing the ocean—are in plain view of the meadow. Up on the hill, however, sites tend to be shady, with sunlight filtered through the trees, so that daylight in the houses must be designed for. Since houses on the hill are so little exposed to general view—in contrast to those on the meadow—forms are often more complex. The overriding character is, nevertheless, simple. The owners of this house, a retired couple, had lived for several years at The Sea Ranch in one of the "Binker Barns" designed by William Turnbull and Charles Moore (page 142) coming to know and appreciate the exceptional quality of the original Sea Ranch buildings and to want the same quality in their new house. The house is simple and unpretentious, reminiscent of The Sea Ranch vernacular but individual in its handling of details and forms. The sloping site allowed for placement of garage, shop and storage under the main house with a minimum disturbance of grade. This gives living areas just enough elevation to afford some view of Black Point and the ocean and, through the trees, of a meadow on the south. Guest rooms are separate from the main house in a compact and appropriately simple unit on the same level as the house. The main living space is open and light, with large windows on two sides and additional light from a monitor window above.

RESIDENCE FOR MR. AND MRS. HENRY O. WHITESIDE, The Sea Ranch, California. Architect: *Donald Jacobs.* Contractor: *Custom Builders, Inc.*

The sculptural forms of the charred remains of old tree stumps, retained and incorporated into the design, are a feature of the entrance to the house. Logs of various lengths, set vertically beside steps from driveway to entrance, further emphasize the woody character of the place. Very few living trees were removed to make way for the house, so during most of the day, sunlight reaches the house through the trees. To bring in as much daylight as possible to entry and dining area, a kind of "light tower" was placed over the entry (across page, top and bottom). Light from its high monitor window (see section) bounces against the opposite wall and ricochets across to dining area.

10

Merg Ross photos

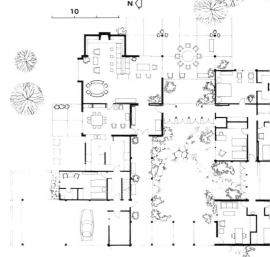

On an upland meadow south of Yosemite, architect John Rex and his family planned a house that serves as the nucleus of a working cattle ranch. The house rests gently on a carpet of wildflowers, and is built around an entry court landscaped in stone, gravel and tufted greenery. If the court is stylistically mannered, it is also conceived and executed with loving attention to detail. The specimen boulders, pitted and covered with lichen, were assembled from various locations around the ranch and placed with evident care. Blocks of bedrooms on the south side of the court are linked to each other and the rest of the house by covered walks that are closed in winter and used as hothouses. In summer, these corridors are thrown open to a prevailing westerly that is funneled through the court to the covered terrace (see plan).

The living room, zoned informally for small and large groupings, opens to the north and southeast to frame wide-angle views of mountain and meadow. The whole scheme is visually unified by a continuous flat roof that keeps the silhouette low and contrasts with the distant Sierras.

Principal materials are slump stone and resawn cedar inside and out. Floors are finished in custom tiles colored to match the surrounding soil.

RESIDENCE FOR MR. AND MRS. JOHN REX, North Forks, California. Architects: *Honnold and Rex;* engineer: *Greve & O'Rourke;* landscape architect: *Edward Huntsman-Trout;* interior design: *Guy Moore and Associates;* contractor: *F. D. Wilcox.*

Leland Lee photos

In the kitchen (above) which opens into the family room, meals can be prepared for as many as one hundred guests. Photo (below) shows corridor buttoned up for winter. Bedroom (left) has its own entrance and opens generously to a view of country once inhabited by Mono Indians.

Entry court, designed to be contemplated rather than used, looks well from all angles and at all seasons. Rock and plant materials are all native to the ranch.

Living room sub-divides easily to accommodate groups of various sizes. A small alcove with its fireplace provides an intimate setting for winter evenings. Ceiling height is raised to 16 feet over the rest of the room and furnishes entertainment space at a grander scale. Couches are covered in cowhide and all accent colors are chosen to match local wildflowers that bloom in profusion each spring.

INDEX